COMFORT ZONE
INVESTING

How to Tailor Your Portfolio for High Returns and Peace of Mind

Gillette Edmunds

 CAREER PRESS

THE CAREER PRESS, INC.

COMFORT ZONE INVESTING
EDITED BY DIANNA WALSH
TYPESET BY STACEY A. FARKAS
Cover design by Design Concept
Printed in the U.S.A. by Book-mart Press

To order this title, please call toll-free 1-800-CAREER-1 (NJ and Canada: 201-848-0310) to order using VISA or MasterCard, or for further information on books from Career Press.

The Career Press, Inc., 3 Tice Road, PO Box 687,
Franklin Lakes, NJ 07417
www.careerpress.com

Library of Congress Cataloging-in-Publication Data

Edmunds, Gillette.
    Comfort zone investing : how to tailor your portfolio for high returns and peace of mind
/ by Gillette Edmunds
    p. cm.
    Includes index.
    ISBN 1-56414-591-3 (paper)
    1.Portfolio management. 2. Investments. I. Title.

HG4529.5 .E36 2002
332.6—dc21   2001058287

Acknowledgments

Thanks to Kathleen, Jesse, Ellis, and Oliver for being there always and especially when I emerged exhausted from the office.

Thanks to Tom for support, encouragement, editing, and acceptance.

Thanks to Jim, Carol, Jeff, and Kathleen, who took the time to read and edit.

Thanks to Al, Chris, John, Dave, and innumerable anonymous others who hung in there with me during the early drafts and the dark daze of the lawsuit and the happy days that follow.

Thanks to Jim, Rachel, and Elaine, who got more than an earful about the first book and kept coming back for more.

Thanks to Charlie, Duke, Ed, Ted, Rich, Kathy, and my other business associates over the years.

Thanks to everyone who shared with me the truth about their investment fears.

Thanks to Ed Knappman, my agent, and everybody at Career Press.

Thanks to H.P.

CONTENTS

STEP 1
LEARN HOW INVESTMENTS TRIGGER EMOTIONS 29

Chapter 3
Emotional Traps? What Emotional Traps?

Chapter 4
Savings

Chapter 5
Think Twice, Feel Twice, Before You Invest

Chapter 6

Chapter 7

STEP 2
LEARN WHO YOU ARE AS AN INVESTOR 161

Chapter 8

Chapter 8, *cont.*

STEP 3

CHAPTER 1

THE PROBLEM: BAD RESULTS IN GOOD AND BAD MARKETS

*C*omfort zone investing is satisfying and profitable. Getting to your comfort zone is a simple three-step process:

1. Learn how investments trigger emotions.
2. Learn who you are as an investor.
3. Match yourself and compatible investments.

Once you have discovered your comfort zone, returns will be high and investing will not cause you emotional distress.

If you do not know what your comfort zone is, it may be less stressful to spend your excess cash on a trip to Hawaii than to invest it in a popular tax advantaged asset such as a 401(k) stock fund.

The purpose of investing is not to make you miserable. The purpose is to increase the sense of security, serenity, and satisfaction in your life. Therefore, compatibility is important, maybe even more important than return on investments.

Investors who find real estate within their comfort zone will do very well with it, regardless of market conditions. Investors who are emotionally compatible with stocks can be equally successful in the stock market.

Today's most respected investment brand name is U.S. stocks. The stock index fund in a tax-deferred 401(k) is considered a sure thing by the public and investment professionals alike. Studies show that consumers remain loyal to their purchases despite mounting evidence of mediocre and poor performance. To their detriment, real estate buyers remained loyal to real estate until the final crash in the early 1990s. This emotional mistake is being repeated today. Today even behavioral economists invested in the stock market defend stocks as the only asset class for long-term investors. Today everybody is supposed to have the right emotional makeup to invest in stocks. Everybody doesn't.

Investing is a long-term relationship

We are all in a long-term relationship with our investments. Everyone needs to save for retirement. Those who don't are in a negative relationship, which has emotional consequences just like an active relationship.

Active retirement investors must save for 30 or more years to be able to retire comfortably. Then they must invest another 30 or more years in retirement to live comfortably off their investments. If a retirement investor cannot handle the stress of investing in the stock market, yet continues to put most of his savings in the stock market, he will be miserable before and during retirement even if he is financially able to retire on a large nest egg.

For other savers, just the thought of investing makes them nervous. Opening an investment book in the bookstore causes sweaty palms. "Too much information, too much information," their brains scream and they head for another section.

Many people will tell you that investing is not that challenging. "Just buy good stocks and hold them for the long run." Are they telling the whole story? Just holding stocks for the long run can be extremely painful when markets crash, everyone else is selling, family and friends are telling you to get out, and your commissioned broker has better ideas for you while you wait out the storm.

To save for retirement and invest in retirement with equanimity, you must be able to handle all aspects of the investment relationship. There will be rough spots for everyone.

Who owns your investments?

All investments have emotionally trying elements. It is not possible for a human being to invest unemotionally.

Every investment involves adversarial relationships in whole or in part. This explains some of the stress. If you feel like it is an emotional battleground trying to make money investing, you are right; it is. Winning the battle financially can be just as draining as losing.

Adversarial relationships are built into most investment transactions. Stockbrokers, realtors, and insurance salespersons are not bad people out to rip you off. Most are honest and hard-working. However, their livelihood requires that they extract fees from you whether you are aware of this or not. Once you understand all the fees, both up-front and hidden, you can make a decision as to whether or not these fees are money well spent or exorbitant. Unfortunately, it is likely you are unaware of both the hidden fees and the adversarial relationship you have with investment professionals.

Hiring a personal money manager is not the way out either. Some charge hefty fees; require huge minimums; invest to preserve their fees instead of growing your portfolio; and spend a lot of time either on their own portfolio or trying to sell their money management business to a big mutual fund house for a killing, none of which benefits you.

Investing outside the stock market does not solve the problem either. Insurance and annuity companies' main interest is in capturing your funds so they, not you, can profit from investing them. I doubt any insurance representatives will be recommending this book.

Your adversarial relationship is not just with the investment community. You had to wrestle your investment funds away from the boss, the clients, the customers, the source. This money had scars on it before you thought about investing it. Then the Internal Revenue Service (IRS) and the state and city and county took their piece, and left you with two choices. Go to Hawaii or save for your retirement, house, car, children, or some acutely responsible reason. Or you could slip the money into a 401(k), IRA, or Keogh plan, avoiding the taxes and the trip to Hawaii. Great choice. Now you don't get to touch the money for years, unless you are willing to cough up huge penalties, and even when you do get your hands on it in your dotage, you will still pay taxes on it. Investing is fun? Who came up with that idea?

This would all be very simple if you were financially secure.

Are you financially secure?

Take note, this is a trick question. The answer has nothing to do with how much money you have. Consider a question about your relationship with stocks.

Are you and the stock market miserable together?

Your friend Martha says to you, "My husband and I are selling all our shares of Microsoft and buying an elegant six-bedroom house on the 18th green for cash." How do you respond?

1. Rage.
2. Congratulations, I am so happy for you and Joe.
3. Maybe I'll do the same with my Coca-Cola shares.
4. I'll never talk to her again.
5. I'm divorcing my husband. He spends all our money on losing investments, computer gadgets, and junk, and then takes out second mortgages.
6. Our real estate is doing well. It's good to see you are getting smart and putting some money into real estate, even if it is only an overpriced house.
7. How could two idiots like Martha and Joe have bought Microsoft when my husband with an MBA puts everything in some plodding 401(k) mutual funds?
8. Most of the above.
9. All of the above, though several are just fantasies.

Compare this with your emotional maturity regarding marriage. You have been married happily for five years. Your friend Martha says to you, "I think I have finally found the right guy. Joe and I are engaged." You respond:

1. I'm so happy for you. You deserve to have finally found the right guy.
2. I'm so happy for me. I'm glad that issue has been settled in my life for a long time.
3. Both.

Most people have less reaction to Martha's engagement than to Martha's financial windfall. Investing triggers many emotions. Relationships often trigger fewer emotions. Most people have spent time working on their romantic and spousal relationships. Few people have worked on their investment relationships. This would not matter, except that, *as you approach retirement, your relationship to your investments becomes a major relationship in your life.*

Investing triggers many emotions

To be comfortable saving for retirement and spending savings in retirement, your investments must satisfy both your financial and emotional needs. When your investments are lucrative, but you and your investments are not emotionally compatible, you will either get rid of them and look for something new and possibly more incompatible or stew in your misery. Yet it is difficult to even know what your needs are in this relationship.

You are subject to great cultural pressure today to own U.S. stocks, especially the latest fad stocks. It is not just that everybody at the office claims to own them and is checking the results online all day. There are whole institutions devoted to this: CNBC, *The Nightly Business News*, *The Wall Street Journal*, a thousand Web sites, and chat rooms. The pressure to own stocks so you can converse about them is high. But are you happy with them? Is anybody happy with them? How many of your colleagues have stopped to ask what their emotional needs are in their investment relationships? Do they act like they know what their emotional needs are?

Let's return to the question that started this chapter and look at the emotional dilemma apart from the financial. What emotions are triggered by having to choose between retirement savings and vacations? Do you find yourself feeling guilty when you go to Hawaii instead of putting the money in an IRA? Or do you get depressed when you cannot go to Hawaii because all your extra savings are tied up in IRAs and other retirement plans?

Investment compatibility becomes a possibility when you first admit that investing triggers difficult emotions. Try this series of questions and see if you relate to any part of the emotional dilemma:

◆ Have you ever found yourself losing sleep over the market, angry with your broker, unsatisfied with your returns, yet unable to pull out of the market?

◆ Are you jealous of your business associate who has turned it all over to a money manager and has no idea how he is doing?

◆ Does the woman across the street with her string of single-family houses irritate you?

- How did you react when that 35-year-old coworker retired?
- Do you value honesty yet find you have lied to several people about your investments and investment returns?
- Do you seek serenity over financial security?
- Will high returns bring you serenity or just increase your craving for more high returns?

The more you look at it, the more emotionally charged investing becomes. Financial advisors discuss risk as risk of losing money. Isn't the real risk emotional? If you are not in the stock market, you risk being an outcast at the beach gatherings this summer. But if you are in the market, you risk losing sleep and losing time trying to keep up with how you are doing, how the market is doing, and how well everyone else is doing compared to how you are doing.

If you knew yourself better and knew more about the emotional aspects of different investments, investing would be more satisfying. Try this question. Is it easiest for you to trust people, financial markets, or the U.S. Treasury?

Those who have a hard time trusting people will find that turning their assets over to a money manager or a stockbroker creates fear. Many independent business people founded and built up their own businesses because they only really trust themselves. That is fine. If you are like that, yet you have turned your money over to a money manager, you will be uncomfortable even if the money manager produces outstanding financial results. You will be happier making all your own investment decisions even if it costs you money.

Some people cannot trust financial markets. Perhaps you saw your parents lose a fortune in stocks. In that case, you may be more comfortable receiving interest payments from Treasury bonds, even if you could make more money in stocks.

Risk tolerance: The sales tool

Some investment promoters claim they have all this covered. They ask you a series of questions about your risk tolerance before they sell you their products:

- "If the market declines 25 percent in one year, will you take your money out?"

◆ "Are you able to keep the long-term in mind when markets fluctuate or are you more comfortable with investments that do not fluctuate?"

These tests determine your so-called "risk tolerance." Risk tolerance is your ability to handle volatility. Risk tolerance tests are supposed to match you to compatible investments. Unfortunately, they don't.

Risk tolerance is not a good measure of investment compatibility. At best, it measures a narrow aspect of your personality: your theoretical ability to handle volatility. Even if your broker happens to sell the product that is theoretically right for your risk profile and you buy it, studies show that how people think they will react under adverse market conditions and how they actually react are quite different. In fact, few of us know ourselves well enough to know how we would really react in future unknown situations.

The real problem is that risk tolerance tests do not touch the crucial issues: who you are as an investor and how investments interact with your personality. For example, they do not address the issue of the adverse relationships you have with the investment seller and others. In fact, they disguise this issue. These tests lead you to believe that you and the salesperson have the same interest. The tests do not address the issue of overconfidence. Overconfident investors believe they have high risk tolerance when they do not. The tests do not address the issue of people pleasing. People pleasers are often aware that they have low risk tolerance but they buy high risk investments to make their broker or their coworkers happy. In fact, risk tolerance tests do not accurately address any of the issues that will lead you to purchase incompatible investments.

Risk tolerance tests are equally ineffective for average personalities and for extreme personalities such as workaholics, gamblers, and compulsive debtors. Extreme personalities typically have little or no self-knowledge. They will fill out risk profiles identical to those of average investors. Yet once sold an investment product, they will abuse it to a degree unimaginable by the average public. Risk tolerance tests do not pick up money addicts of any kind and lead to no help for these people or those affected by them.

While money addiction is more prevalent in our society than most people realize, the vast majority of investors suffer from less extreme forms of investment incompatibility. The more common symptoms include loss of sleep, irritability, unexplained anger or depression, random resentments, a sense that investing is meaningless, money arguments with a spouse or partner that neither can comprehend, a dim view of retirement possibilities, and a thousand forms of fear.

The major investment fears are that you do not have enough investments now, won't have enough in the future, or will lose what you already have. Then these fears lead to further fears. If you don't have enough savings, then how could you have enough money for travel, clothes, restaurants, a new car, a better house, a real life? Or you fear you cannot and will not ever grasp the mathematical complexities of compound interest and probability theory and you cannot trust those who do understand these concepts. Then there is the underlying fear that investing is irrational and no amount of study will help.

The premise of this book is that these feelings and fears are normal and healthy; understanding them and understanding the emotional hooks of different investments will lead to a greater sense of peace and contentment in your life. They don't sell peace and contentment on Wall Street. You have to find it within yourself first and then look for the investments that enhance it, rather than disturb it.

When you know more about yourself and about the products that are out there, no risk tolerance tests with hidden agendas will sell you incompatible investments anymore. Investing will become an area of great satisfaction in your life.

CHAPTER 2

THE SOLUTION: INVEST WITHIN YOUR COMFORT ZONE

*Y*ou are not guaranteed high returns from any investment class over any time period. Hundreds of books proclaim that buy-and-hold investors in the U.S. stock market will reap high returns. However, check the disclaimers in the front of the books. The author is not guaranteeing anything. The same claims were made about Japanese stocks in 1989. More than a decade later, buy-and-hold investors in Japanese stock have lost more than two-thirds of their money.

While no asset class is guaranteed to provide gains over any time period, the wrong asset class, even if the returns are positive, can drive you nuts. If you invest within your comfort zone, your enjoyment of life will improve as your ability to handle both gains and losses improves.

Comfort zone investing is...

Comfort zone investing consists of knowledge of how different investments affect your emotions, knowledge of who you are in relation to investments, and choosing investments that match your personality.

The comfort zone is tested most often by large increases and decreases in investment values. Studies of stock investors show that most investors react to declines in stock values by holding on too long-hoping the price will improve. Investors also sell winners too soon to lock-in profits, missing even greater gains, and avoid purchases of bargain stocks that have declined in price fearing the declines will continue indefinitely. The net result is individual and professional investors consistently fail to make even half the stock market averages.

Many studies describe these phenomena. These self-defeating behaviors are attributed to thinking patterns such as "loss aversion," the "disposition effect," and "mental accounting." Unfortunately, the studies only describe the patterns and the resulting low returns. The studies do not tell you why you are reacting dysfunctionally nor how to act maturely.

This book answers both questions. The comfort zone has three elements: self-knowledge, investment knowledge, and matching yourself to the proper investments. If any of these three elements is out of place, your reaction to your investments will be dysfunctional. If you are in the right investments, you will act maturely. For example, many investors think that investing is solely about numbers. Unfortunately, focusing on numbers ignores both who you are and the nature of investments.

Investing is not about numbers

Few investors realize that investing is not a numbers game. Making buy-and-sell decisions based solely on price movements is a strong indication you are outside your comfort zone. Buy at 5 and sell at 10 or buy at 10 and sell at 5 is trouble both financially and emotionally. Buy-and-sell decisions need to be made on the basis of knowledge of who you are as an investor, a fundamental understanding of the investment, and a determination of whether the underlying fundamentals of the investment meet your investment needs. If a company or mutual fund is having a bad quarter or a bad year or a great quarter or a great year, you need to understand how it is reacting to that situation and if its reaction indicates that it fits your investment needs. Price movements are external factors that tell you little about the company, the mutual fund, or yourself.

An emotionally mature adult would not make personal relationship decisions based solely on external factors. If you are in a new romantic relationship and your lover's mother suddenly dies, do you end the relationship immediately (sell) or watch how your lover reacts to the loss of a mother and watch how you react to your lover's loss. If your lover then inherits half a million dollars, do you make a decision to marry (buy) or do you watch how your lover reacts to new wealth and how you react to your lover's financial gain. In a romantic relationship, your goal is to build a long-term positive relationship. Breaking up or staying together based on external factors such as a death or inheritance is clearly immature. The internal factors, your lover's emotional development and your own, are the real basis for judging the long-term potential for marriage or a parting. The internal factors, your emotional makeup and investment policy, and the company's reaction to success or failure, are the real basis to determine buy-and-sell decisions.

Investing outside the comfort zone is exemplified by basing trading decisions solely on price. Other external factors also influence investors when they are outside their comfort zone. Consider the example of Michael and Susan.

Michael and Susan

Michael and Susan have been saving for retirement for 10 years. They are also, like all the characters in this book, a composite from interviews and people I have worked with during the past 21 years. Since Michael's major promotion 10 years ago, they have invested about $50,000 a year. Prior to that, they had less than $10,000 in investments. Now, stockbrokers, realtors, insurance salespeople, venture capitalists, hedge fund vendors, and other investment product peddlers have their number and routinely call them.

Michael and Susan have compiled investments worth $450,000 during the past 10 years: half in a 401(k) and half in an online brokerage account. Immediately, you might notice the math. If they have invested $50,000 a year for the past 10 years, achieving a zero total return on their money, they should have $500,000 in investments. You might do the math, but Michael and Susan have not. You would also think that Michael and Susan would be happy with the size of their nest egg. Sill in their mid-40s, they are in the top 1 percent of wealth in the world. But they are miserable.

Michael losses sleep over his investments regularly. Though he works 60 hours a week, he finds time several months a year to shift between $100,000 and $300,000 from one investment fad to another, believing he will increase his returns and then be happier with his portfolio. Among the other high-income employees where he works, this is routine practice. In fact, the main non-work-related topic among these employees is investing. Though not one of them has ever calculated their annual returns, they all constantly chase high returns and lose sleep worrying about the market.

Susan, a stay-at-home mom and part-time consultant, is equally un-happy with their investments. She wants Michael to work less, even take early retirement, and consult part-time so he does not miss his children's childhood years. She is certain they were happier before Michael's big promotion. She is angry that their portfolio is in constant flux. She has no understanding of why one year they seem to have all their money in small cap stocks, the next year in municipal bonds, then in tech stocks, and now in hedge funds. She is convinced that they are on the verge of losing it all any minute and she will have to go to work full-time.

You might think the case of Michael and Susan is unusual. It is not. Studies by Dalbar Inc. and others show that as many as 90 percent of individual investors underperform stock market averages because they buy and sell too often. In fact, studies by Brad M. Barber, Terrance Odean, Moringstar, and others have shown that individual investors make returns about half as high as the stock market. During 1970-2000 period when the market made 12 percent a year, individual investors made 6 percent. Indi-viduals even underperformed the bond market by a significant margin. How-ever, hiring professional money management does not solve the problem. Studies by Mark Hulbert and others show that professional money manag-ers also trade too often and underperform the stock market 80 percent of the time. Unfortunately, all these studies focus on investment return.

Intelligence does not determine investment results

The implication of these studies is that individual investors and profes-sional money managers are emotionally and intellectually dumb when it comes to stock market investing. If they were smarter, they would at mini-mum buy and hold the market index.

Emotional and intellectual intelligence has nothing to do with this inabil-ity of investors in stocks to keep pace with the market. After all, marketing studies show most investors are of average or better intellectual intelli-gence. Statistically, it is unlikely that 80 percent of any large group is below average in any area. What is more likely is that a large percentage of the underperformers, both professional and amateur, are emotionally and intel-lectually healthy but do not have the emotional makeup to be investing in stocks. Investor's who would thrive with tax lien certificates or real estate investment trusts (REITs) have been diverted into the stock market by the mass publicity machine of Wall Street. After all, every study I have seen shows that 10 percent or more of people have the emotional and intellectual makeup to thrive in the stock market. It is the failure of these studies to set out better alternatives for the rest of investors that this book remedies.

Emotional compatibility is not a statistic within a range that incorporates the entire population such as an intelligence quota (IQ). It is a matching process. In relationships, each unique individual is matched with another unique individual. There are many types out there. If you find yourself always with the wrong type, get help.

The same is true for investment compatibility. There are hundreds of asset classes. Step 1 discusses the emotional implications of all the major and many minor investment classes. Fortunately, if you find yourself incompatible with the stock market, the chances of finding better investment satisfaction elsewhere are high. In the case of Michael and Susan, once they work on their investment maturity, they will find many asset classes that suit them better than stocks.

Michael and Susan's solution

Michael tinkers with his portfolio obsessively. In prior years, he read investment magazines and newspapers late into the night. Now he has a fast Internet connection and often signs off after midnight. Susan is freaked out by the paper gains and losses that routinely occur every month. The abstract nature of the account statements, reports, newspaper articles, and Web sites makes her nervous. Her mind cannot grasp what they really own nor does she understand why Michael is constantly playing with it. Ever since the decline of 1990, when they were new to the stock market, there has been a sense of impending doom over their financial security.

Interestingly, Michael and Susan would both be happier with a portfolio primarily consisting of single-family homes. Michael's tinkering could cut costs and improve rents and tenant quality. He has no guilt about being a landlord. He and Susan have a nice house they are proud to own. They are now living in their third home together. Together they were able to buy two cute cottages in attractive neighborhoods, which they sold for much more than the purchase price. Michael is fair with the many employees he supervises. There is no reason he would be a poor landlord. Michael is also not likely to trade properties. While he is able to justify many small commissions to a discount broker, having never added them all up, the idea of giving 6 percent of his property to a Realtor every time he sells a building does not appeal to him. Susan could drive by and look at their properties any time she needed reassurance. The children could help out cleaning and fixing up between tenants. Though Michael may lose a major topic of conversation at the office, he would sleep better and be more productive at work. He would also be wealthier. If, in each of the last 10 years, he had bought a new single family home with $50,000 down, putting nothing in his 401(k) or anywhere else, he could potentially have equity of $1,000,000 today.

Ten years ago Michael looked at both real estate and stocks. A stock-broker told him that real estate was too complex. Because stocks and stock mutual funds were simple and easy to understand, he would do better in the stock market. Ironically, in 10 years of study, Michael still does not grasp all the complexities of the stock market; yet with no study, he and Susan were able to purchase three homes. The value of his current home has far out-performed his stock investments.

Despite his own experience, Michael still believes that real estate is too complex and the stock market is relatively simple. In fact, more than 100 factors can influence the price of a stock, whereas less than six factors affect the price of real estate. At first, real estate investing appears complex. After a year or two, it becomes simple. Stocks and stock mutual funds, a first glance, seem simple. After a year or two, the complexities appear. After a decade, the complexities of stock and stock mutual fund investing can become overwhelming. Late-night online investors, including Michael, come to understand why veteran stock managers work 80-hour weeks.

So how do Michael and Susan move out from under their defended position in the stock market and into their comfort zone of real estate? Financially, this can easily be accomplished. In fact, they have so few gains in their taxable portfolio, they will not pay any taxes to shift into real estate. They will get tax deductions from selling out. Considering the negative investment returns they have been getting in the stock market, it also would be reasonable to take a 10 percent penalty and liquidate their 401(k). But emotionally, Michael and Susan are attached to their dysfunctional relationship with the stock market.

A dysfunctional relationship between a person and an inanimate object?

Investment relationships are not identical to romantic, family, and social relationships solely among people. Though people, often with conflicting interests, are involved in investment relationships, the primary relationship is between the individual and an inanimate object: money. At first, it may seem odd that a relationship between a person and an inanimate object could be dysfunctional. In fact, our society is saturated with such dysfunctional relationships.

It is estimated that 10 percent to 15 percent of the U.S. population is alcoholic; essentially more than 30 million Americans have a life threatening dysfunctional relationship to an inanimate object: alcohol. One out of every three adult Americans are obese, based on their dysfunctional relationship to food. Sixty million American families have larger credit card debt than they can afford. Their relationship to material goods is dysfunctional. In fact, consumerism dysfunction has reached new heights. Compulsive shopping is portrayed in the media as fun, not as an illness. Yet in the booming economy with a roaring stock market of the late 1990s, the number of personal bankruptcies had never been higher: 331,000 filed for bankruptcy in 1980; 413,000 in 1985; 783,000 in 1990; 927,000 in 1995; and more than 1,300,000 filed in 2000. In recent years, Americans as a whole have spent 1 percent more than they earn.

Process addiction is also on the rise in many parts of our society. Workaholism is rampant. Little mention is made in the press of the effects on children and spouse of the missing dad or mom or the fortunes lost in worthless companies and the resultant grief, alcoholism, drug addiction, and suicide. Sex addiction is portrayed as fun on cable and the Web; broken homes, AIDS, and herpes are yesterday's news. In a society like this, the day trading addiction is hardly newsworthy. Stock market obsession is considered harmless. Yet if you bought this book, you must be feeling some pain around your investing. The good news is, there is a way out.

A simple, commonsense solution

For more than 65 years there has been a simple, commonsense solution. In 1935, Bill Wilson, a pioneer of U.S. stock analysis, and Dr. Bob Smith, a medical doctor, developed a treatment for addiction to inanimate objects and processes. This treatment, known as the 12-steps, was originally only applied to alcohol addiction. Today, this treatment is used to correct dysfunctional relationships to work, credit cards, sex, drugs, and money. It has helped me in my investment relationships and I have seen it help hundreds of others. I will show you how it can help you determine who you are in relation to investments and how to pick investments that fit your emotional makeup.

The approach I suggest is simple and straightforward. It is equally effective for an investor with $1,000 or $10,000,000. No college education is required. No miracles are necessary. You will not have to examine childhood family issues around money, achieve ever higher stages of emotional maturity, sit in odd positions and chant, have courage or a spiritual awakening, or do anything weird. All those activities are fine and helpful in many aspects of life, but that is not what is necessary here. You will look at your history investing, write down and organize your experience in designated categories to see what happened internally, and learn from your experience. No expensive seminar is required. The price of this book, something to write on, and a co-participant are all you need.

The 3 steps

To get from the chaos of your investment life to your comfort zone, you need to take three steps: study the emotional content of different investments, study your own emotional makeup, and match your emotional makeup to the appropriate investments.

To avoid confusion, I have divided this book into three steps rather than three parts:

Step 1: Chapters 3 through 7 set out the emotional content of the different investments. Step 1 requires study but no writing or analysis. The material in Step 1 will also be used as a reference when you reach Step 3. Per the discussion in Step 1, saving, investing, and speculating are different activities. However, throughout this book, the term "investor" is used to signify a person engaged in all three activities unless otherwise specified. The term "investment" also includes savings, investments, and speculations unless clarified. Among other things, Step 1 is about learning the difference between a saver, an investor, and a speculator.

Step 2: Chapter 8 shows you how to study your emotional makeup. It requires writing and analysis. Step 2 is the workbook section of *Comfort Zone Investing*.

Step 3: Chapters 9 matches you to the appropriate investments.

Michael and Susan can move from the chaos of their current investment life to owning single family homes by following these three steps:

1. First, they need to study the material in Step 1. This will show them the range of possible investments. Investments are divided into three broad categories: savings, investments, and speculations. Michael and Susan will quickly realize that they are neither pure savers nor pure speculators. Their comfort zone is likely to be in the investment category. They are advised to skim Chapter 4, study Chapter 5 closely, and skip Chapter 6.

2. Second, they need to work the exercises in Step 2 to learn more about who they are as investors. They currently have too little self-knowledge to determine which asset class in the investment category is best for them. This will require a weekend of writing as explained in Step 2.

3. Third, with their new self-knowledge, they will be able to quickly make the connections suggested in Step 3 and find their comfort zone: single-family rental houses.

The investment emotions inventory

Step 2 explains in detail how you can gain self-knowledge from an emotions inventory. An emotions inventory is similar to a physical inventory of goods in a shop or investments in a portfolio. It is done for the same purpose as well. Goods that are defective must be discovered and discarded; investments that have no future must be liquidated. Emotions that prevent investment compatibility must be recognized and isolated to make room in the psyche for those that are functional. Thereafter you will be investing in your comfort zone.

This simple process has worked for me, an ordinary investor, and it will work for most of you. I do not claim any high level of emotional maturity or spiritual development. No one who knows me would describe me as a saint or a guru. I am not a trained therapist. I do not have an MBA. I am not a Certified Financial Planner, and I am not a Chartered Financial Analyst. After 21 years of living off my investments and taking regular investment emotional inventories, I do know which investments work best with my personality and which investments irritate me or keep me awake at night. By staying in my comfort zone, investing is fun for me. It will be fun for you too, though you may not see that yet.

The misery of repeated, painful investment mistakes will be over and creativity and joy will grow in your life.

Michael and Susan are typical of investors who need to take an inventory. They know something is not working in their investment lives. As yet, they cannot pin down the nature of the problem or the solution. Though many of their friends and co-workers are aware of Michael and Susan's specific character flaws, Michael and Susan themselves are unaware. A weekend working through the exercises in Chapter 8 will change their lives. Once they find their comfort zone, other aspects of their life will improve as well. Their children will be integrated into their investment life. Their investment life will improve their marriage rather than be a source of division.

Self-acceptance, not self-improvement

Comfort zone investing does not mean you become a flawless investor or a spiritual giant. For most people, striving for financial maturity is a process of self-discovery and self-acceptance, not a process of self-improvement.

To achieve serenity in investing, once you know how you relate to different investments, you do not have to change who you are; you simply need to change your investments to fit you. Often in marriage or work relationships, you must change yourself if you are to be happy, because your spouse or boss is not about to change. Changing yourself is much more difficult and painful than changing your investments.

Changing investments is not, however, entirely cost free. Switching from stocks to real estate, for example, incurs taxes, commissions, closing fees, research, and assessment hours, as well as other monetary, time, and effort costs. There are social costs as well. You may have to reach outside office norms to find what works for you. If you are a real estate guy and the firm only offers 401(k)s with no REIT option and lots of free company stock, you might have to explain to your colleagues why you put nothing in the plan and spend weekends driving around looking at shopping centers.

Investment bigamy is fine

Fortunately, comfort zone investing does not require you to be as strait-laced as relationship maturity might. Unlike marriage, multiple partners are fine in investing. Just be sure you know your needs and which investments fill those needs. If your need to conform at work is strong but you also know you need investments that you can drive by and look over now and then, there is nothing wrong with having money in both the 401(k) and rental houses. A mix of biotech stocks for excitement, real estate to tinker, and bonds for stability is fine if that fits your requirements. The trick is to get your mix correct.

The self-discovery process described in Step 2 is a powerful tool. Millions of people, including me, have used it to change their lives for the better. Combined with the knowledge of emotional triggers for different classes of investment set out in Step 1, you will be able to dramatically improve your satisfaction from investing.

This is a long-term process and you will be asked to repeat the steps outlined in Chapter 9 at least annually as your financial circumstances change over the years. However, if you have thoroughly worked the program outlined in this book and continue to be unhappy with your investments, do not be discouraged. The program in this book will teach you who you are in relation to investments, how to accept yourself as that person, and what investments work for that person. If nothing works for the person you discover yourself to be or if you cannot discover yourself in this process, then it is necessary to change yourself. Sometimes your investments are not wrong; instead, you need a new way to look at your investments and you need to give yourself the gift of getting those new glasses.

True money addicts need additional help

The process of discovering who you are in relation to investments is different for everybody. We all start at different places based on our genetic makeup, our childhood, and our good or bad fortune, we move through different experiences in life, and arrive at different places. This book does not claim that this simple three-step program is the only process of achieving emotional compatibility with your investments. These three steps are helpful for most people and have certainly been helpful for me.

If you have severe money dysfunction, realize that you are not likely to accept that immediately. One of the prevailing characteristics of all addiction is that the addict does not believe he or she has a problem. Everyone around him, except coaddicts, believes he has problems, but the addict himself considers his behavior normal. If you work through the exercises in this book, yet you still have a sense of impending doom around your investments, get further help. The answer is out there for you; it is just beyond the scope of this book.

The more difficult personal change process

The personal change process is harder than the process described in this book. Outside help is necessary. You deserve to have a happy investment life just as you deserve to have a happy relationship. To achieve personal change, you can commit yourself to a codependence treatment program, see a psychiatrist, take prescribed medication, go to a trained psychologist or therapist, attend group psychotherapy, commit to Gamblers Anonymous, and enlist the support of family, friends, and work colleagues. But you must get help. You cannot fix yourself. You cannot use a broken tool to fix a broken tool. The input of trained professionals and those who have recovered is absolutely necessary.

For most of you, however, Step 1 is the entryway to your comfort zone.

STEP 1

Learn How Investments Trigger Emotions

*I*nvestors need to know their limits. In some ways, investing is like driving. Risks must be balanced with rewards.

All drivers know that the faster you go, the sooner you get there, unless you run off the road or get ticketed or die in a car wreck. Speed must be balanced with safety. After years of driving, several tickets, and a few wrecks and near misses, most drivers know their limits. Some drivers are comfortable in the fast lane, yet slow down to the posted speed limit on exit ramps. Other drivers like the slow lane, but leave the motor running when filling up the tank. The raging driver is only happy on the road honking and flipping people off while the ultracautious never drive at night or on freeways. Ultimately, arriving faster is a secondary goal for most drivers.

Investments are touted for their high returns. Investors must balance return with anxiety and other emotions. High return often entails high anxiety, and low return usually means low anxiety. However, investing is complex. Some investments have high returns with complexity and low anxiety. Investors who can handle complexity will be happy. Other investors will be miserable. Some investments offer high returns with extensive effort. Some low-return investments entail an emotional roller coaster. Extreme speculation sometimes leads to gambling addiction. Some investors can handle a multitude of investments, and other investors are only comfortable with one asset class.

How to use the material in Step 1

Step 1 shows you how investments trigger emotions. It contains more information than most readers will need to find their comfort zone.

Chapter 3 introduces investment emotions. All readers should study this chapter.

Chapters 4, 5, and 6 explain the emotional triggers from savings, investments, and speculations. Read the introduction to each of these chapters and then read the section on any investments that you own or have owned. For example, if you have stocks and corporate bonds and used to own certificates of deposit (CDs), read about stocks and bonds in Chapter 5 and CDs in Chapter 4. Then read about any other investments that interest you. Perhaps you have been hearing a lot about hedge funds, and you have heard good things about REITs, then read about hedge funds in Chapter 6 and about REITs in Chapter 5. Skip or skim any part of Chapters 4, 5, and 6 that do not interest you. You can come back to these chapters later if necessary.

However, everyone should then study Chapter 7, because readers are likely to experience at least one of the issues described in it.

As you read and study the material in Step 1, consider your experience investing so far. Determine what you have learned about your limits. For each investment with which you have no experience, consider if it would challenge your limits as you now see them.

Step 2 will show you more about who you are as an investor, including your limits. Step 3 directs you on how to pick investments described in Step 1 that match your personality.

Though it may seem so at first, this section of the book is not a criticism of the financial services industry. Nor is this an essay calling for changes in the financial services industry. The worst practices of the industry are described so that you can test your ability to deal with these practices. I do not believe the financial services industry needs to change or that any more regulation or legislation of the industry is necessary.

The point of this book is that you need to either adjust to existing practices or switch to other investments that you find more comfortable. There are many investments to choose from. Most investors can find the returns they seek and the comfort level they are hoping for within the existing financial products. Those who cannot find their comfort zone will need to change themselves, not the financial services industry.

EMOTIONAL TRAPS? WHAT EMOTIONAL TRAPS?

*B*efore all the hype about stocks, back in the Dark Ages of investing, novice investors put everything into savings accounts. After a few years of experience, they ventured into the bond market. Five years playing with government bonds led to another five years investing in corporate bonds. Having built up capital and emotional tools, these apprentice investors then bought utility stocks, blue chip stocks, or real estate. Another decade or so and they were ready for speculation in tech stocks, emerging market stocks, commodities, and anything else the markets could throw at them. At each stage of development, the investor learned the emotional twists and turns of investing along with the knowledge of companies and markets.

Today, investors start with tech stocks, possessing little knowledge of companies or markets and never building the emotional skills needed to handle the most challenging investments.

Each stage of investment maturity triggers different emotions. Saving triggers different emotions than investing, which in turn triggers different emotions than speculating.

Some of you have MBAs or CPAs and can quickly pick up company and market data. Others are therapists or trained emotionally to handle conflicts. Most readers are neither. This chapter will define common types of emotional traps you will encounter with investments. Chapters 4, 5, and 6 will show how savings, investments, and speculations trigger emotional reactions. Then, Chapter 7 shows how portfolio structure can twist your emotions. These five chapters will give you the emotional information equivalent to that of a 20-year, full-time investor. Step 2 will raise your level of self-knowledge so that you can determine what investments are appropriate for you.

Pay close attention to the emotional content described in Chapters 3 through 7. Your future sleep is at stake.

The obstacle course overview

Each investment has its own emotional traps. Ancient tribes stored seeds through winter. These tribal savings were loaded with community and individual feelings. Today, few realize the embedded emotion in passbook savings accounts until banks begin to fail or inflation destroys the purchasing power of precious dollars.

Investing produces a wide range of emotion. The highs can be as disorienting as the lows. The most common emotional traps are described here. For each, consider if you would be comfortable owning investments that produce these feelings.

Complete powerlessness

A feeling of complete powerlessness is unusual. We all like to feel that life is moving along in a positive, predictable fashion. For most, a sense of control over his or her own destiny is important. Unfortunately, savings, investing, and speculating are all affected by elements beyond our control. At times, these elements produce extreme results. When the stock market dropped 90 percent between 1929 and 1933, the sense of powerlessness was so great that a whole generation vowed never to buy a single share again. Those left out of the great tech bubble that ended in March 2000 felt equally powerless as they saw friends or acquaintances become instant millionaires. Powerlessness is most extreme in stock investing, but it is found in real estate booms and busts, bond defaults, and other investments.

Powerlessness is paralyzing for the majority of investors. Market shocks cause a few investors to panic; most sit on the sidelines experiencing a sense of powerlessness as prices gyrate wildly. Anxiety, numbness, and depression are common manifestations of the sense of powerlessness.

Panic has a bad reputation as an investment emotion. Brokers, mutual fund companies, journalists, and others who profit from the stock market know that panicked investors often avoid stocks for decades. They portray panic as the worst response to powerlessness in all circumstances. However, panic is a healthy response to many powerless situations. Investors who panicked out of the stock market in 1929 at the low reacted well. The market continued down for three more years and never returned, on a sustained basis, to the 1929 *low* until the early 1950s. Tech investors who listened to the stock promoters and did not panic in April 2000 made a grave error. Many still sit on tech stocks that are worth a fraction of what they were in March 2000.

For the emotionally mature, powerlessness is a relief. There is great freedom in recognizing powerlessness, surrendering, and moving on. For the immature, powerlessness can lead to desperate acts, usually self-destructive. Consider how you react to powerlessness.

Unmanageability

You must also think about unmanageability. A sense of unmanageability is common with investments. The causes of unmanageability are many but usually center around investment professionals and investment institutions. Insurance salespeople may manipulate investors into high-commission, high-surrender fee, and inappropriate variable annuities. The chosen mutual fund might have huge loads and high minimums. The online brokerage Web site may freeze during the market crash.

Unmanageability can also be subtle. For example, savers want to own money market funds in their 401(k) accounts. Often the company will only match their savings with company stock and will encourage them to convert their money market funds into more company stock. Then office politics dictate that anyone wishing to be promoted buy company stock in the 401(k) and accept options on company stock as compensation.

Unmanageable investments gnaw at the investor, often for years or decades. Unmanageability manifests as anger, frustration, and resentment. Stockbrokers confuse investors with lots of numbers and stories and then sell them inappropriate stocks. The investors cannot sue. They were shown prospectuses and all the legal mumblings were made. What is left is a dud stock and a resentment against the broker, the stocks, the brokerage house, and the whole idea of buying stocks.

Typically, the sense of powerlessness leads to passivity. Unmanageability leads to attempts to manage people, institutions, and policies. Change brokers, change stocks, change Realtors, keep it all in a money market account. In the extreme, unmanageability manifests as rage. Investors who shoot their broker, call in bomb threats, plant false rumors on the Internet, or manipulate stock prices are attempting to control unmanageable investments.

Helplessness

It is important to distinguish among a sense of powerlessness, a feeling of unmanageability, and a sense of helplessness. Investors are never helpless. They can always sell the investment or abandon it to bankruptcy and move on. However, many investors feel helpless.

In bubbles and crashes, investors believe they have no choices; they feel helpless but they are not. While you are powerless over the direction of the market and you cannot manage your mutual fund manager, you can sell the mutual fund and invest in real estate.

Saving instruments rarely trigger helplessness. Generally, volatile investments and speculations trigger helplessness.

Helplessness is a false message you tell yourself. All that is necessary is for your mind to convince you that you are stuck. When a stock declines 25 percent, some investors recognize they made a bad investment, take a loss, and invest elsewhere. The helpless investor tells herself that she cannot afford a loss, she must hold on until she gets even. As the loss increases, she rationalizes away all arguments for getting out: people will think I am a bad investor if I lose money here; the tax deduction is too small to be worth anything; I will look stupid for having bought at such a high price; I will be a hero when the stock makes a huge comeback; and so on. Meanwhile, her depression increases. The helpless investor never gets out, riding the stock into bankruptcy if necessary. If you are prone to helplessness, carefully consider if the investments described in Chapters 4, 5, and 6 will trigger your helplessness.

Grandiosity

The opposite extreme from helplessness is grandiosity. Investing commonly triggers grandiosity: a false sense of expertise, manageability, and control. Grandiosity tells you that the investment will work out because *you* invested in it. In the tech bubble, many instant investment geniuses were created. The lone speculator on a winning streak commonly experiences grandiosity.

Some investors get to grandiosity over time. I started out self-assured. A few years of luck led to overconfidence. Investment profits in the millions then turned overconfidence into grandiosity. The crash of 1987 crushed my grandiosity.

Be wary of investing with grandiose money managers and mutual funds. Money managers are particularly prone to grandiosity. A lucky streak or record of excellent returns is not required. Simply controlling $100 million or more leads to challenging emotional traps such as grandiosity. It is my observation that investors with less than 20 years experience are rarely emotionally mature enough to handle large sums of money and the accompanying salaries and bonuses. Mutual fund managers who had more than 30 percent in tech during the tech wreck suffered the ill effects of grandiosity. Many management committees suffer from institutionalized grandiosity. Entire mutual fund families have entrenched grandiosity.

Successful real estate speculation leads to grandiosity. Small real estate investors, who missed the stock bear market of 2000-2001, are prone to grandiosity.

Grandiosity, when returns are positive, manifests as extreme good humor and excitement. Grandiosity can be intoxicating. Once experienced, gamblers seek to recreate the high. Day traders continually believe they will have another streak. Tech investors search for the next Microsoft. Real estate developers crave breaking ground on the next mega project.

Yet, even on a winning streak, grandiosity has a down side. A sense of isolation is common. Sudden wealth stands out in a society where savings are accumulated slowly. Grandiosity can lead to a loss of connection with family, friends, colleagues, social norms, and even one's self.

Grandiosity is often followed by both poor investment results and personal unhappiness. Crashing from grandiosity can be very painful. The detox process leads to grief, sadness, plummeting self-esteem, self-loathing, or depression. Thoughts of suicide are common. Actual suicide is the extreme manifestation of fallen grandiosity.

Although some people are not prone to grandiosity, you should consider any experience you might have with it.

Overconfidence

A lesser form of ego inflation is overconfidence. Overconfidence is your mind telling you that you know what you are doing and that things will work out even though you have little experience and have done little research or investigation. Overconfidence can lead you to trust your own decisions, as well as your advisors, based on flimsy or nonexistent evidence. Overconfident investors fail to scrutinize investment advisors, money managers, mutual fund managers, realtors, journalists, and other supposed experts.

Many people with money to invest suffer from overconfidence. The fact that you have money to invest tells your ego that you have a superior intellect than those who have no money to invest. The mere fact of having money to invest leads you to believe that you will invest it well.

However, overconfidence is not always the result of any prior success or experience. Many investments are sold as simple, easy paths to riches. This triggers overconfidence in inexperienced investors. The notion that stocks are the best investment for the long-term led to overconfidence in stocks for millions of investors. Without challenging this notion, investors shifted money out of bonds and money market funds and into stocks. Overconfident investors failed to ask how long the long-term is. If stocks are a bad investment while you are saving for retirement and a worse investment during your retirement, is it helpful if they are the best investment for the next hundred years after your death?

Overconfidence can become the norm in investment bubbles. Investment experts and the financial press were overconfident in stocks by the end of the 1990s bull market.

Your overconfidence is used against you to sell investment products. If you are a highly competent professional, your ego is likely to convince itself that it is also going to be a highly competent investor. The combination of a Realtor's pitch and a professional's ego has closed many strip shopping center deals.

Any investment can trigger overconfidence if properly presented to the client. Security and Exchange Commission (SEC) rules that only allow certain investments to be sold to investors with large assets or large incomes promote wealthy investors' overconfidence in their ability to invest. Limited partnerships are a typical trigger to overconfidence. High minimum investment amounts and a limited number of shares available only to qualified investors causes many deals to be sold without proper scrutiny.

The press can also lead the masses into overconfidence. *Irrational Exuberance* by Robert Shiller explains in detail how the press, word of mouth, and many other factors created the stock bubble of the late 1990s.

Many academic studies have demonstrated the effects of overconfidence on investors. Despite studying overconfidence, some finance professors never overcome it themselves.

Overconfidence is inevitable in today's world. As workers increasingly specialize and stay busy, it is impossible for them to have the time and expertise necessary to thoroughly investigate investments and investment advisors. However, many investors do not suffer from overconfidence. In fact, lack of confidence is a bigger issue for many. These include people pleasers who rely on others' judgments rather than their own and those who suffer from inferiority, confusion, and an inability to handle any complexity.

Consider whether you are more likely to make mistakes due to over-confidence or lack of confidence.

Inferiority

Investors are intimidated by many investments. Hedge funds are thought to employ exotic strategies that the investor could never understand. Real estate is said to be too difficult for average investors. A feeling of inferiority has channeled many investors away from safe, appropriate investments and into what are marketed as "simple, sure things." The avoidance of real estate in the 1990s due to intimidation by stockbrokers, who labeled it complex, accompanied by the propaganda that stocks required no work and are the best investment for the long run led to much grief in 2000 and 2001.

Confusion

Confusion is built into many aspects of the investment scene. Investors experiencing confusion often shut down or make quick, poor choices.

Stocks are the most confused asset class. Thousands of mutual funds and stocks cause mass confusion. Few people know how to compare all the funds and how to distinguish among all the companies, much less how to fit different funds or stocks with different investment goals and different investors. Many investors buy nothing or buy whatever is most hyped. They are baffled by brokerage statements and tax implications. Few know if they are making money or losing money, much less how they compare to market averages.

While some investment professionals use confusion to sell a product, some are also genuinely confused. Confused advisors give confused advice. For example, many brokers are excellent at customer relations and sales, but inexperienced at economic analysis. Your broker may not understand the correlation of return for different asset classes to different economic conditions including booms, recessions, depressions, high inflation, low inflation, and deflation. Your confusion may be caused by your advisor's confusion.

Confusion is often unexplainable. The A-rated corporation reports record profits each quarter, yet the value of the corporate bonds declines. A REIT cancels the dividend until further notice, but the REIT price doubles. An obscure currency collapses and Ginnie Mae funds decline.

Alternatively, confusion is used as an excuse to avoid change. Confused day traders find they are making more profitable than losing trades, yet their account value declines steadily; however, they continue to trade. Confused 401(k) investors add to their stock mutual funds every year in a bull market, yet their account value is no higher than the total cash contributed to the account; however, they continue to add to the account.

Complexity

Complexity is not an emotion but an intellectual state. Nevertheless, it functions to send many investors outside their comfort zone. Complexity can cause confusion but it is not confusion. Complex investments understood are satisfying for some investors. Most investors, though, prefer simple investments. They have enough complexity in their lives already. Complexity requires work to understand and exploit. Most investors are not looking for mind-twisting experiences.

Complexity comes in three main forms: mathematical, conceptual, and tax related. Some investors are comfortable with mathematical complexity but not conceptual complexity and vice versa. Option strategies involve mathematical complexity. A wide range of calculations must be made to determine the potential outcomes and to hedge each outcome. A salesperson, used to bantering about ideas while the home office calculates profits, may be out of his comfort zone in options. He may, however, enjoy venture capital.

Venture capital requires a wide grasp of ideas and concepts. To determine if gizmo A is a good investment you have to know:

◆ What it does and what is does not do.
◆ What other gizmos are currently available and what they do and what they do not do.
◆ All the other gizmos being developed.
◆ What their prospects are.
◆ The prospects for the industry.
◆ The supply and demand conditions of the industry both current and future.
◆ The financial aspect of all the variables.

An accountant may be out of her comfort zone in venture capital. Her brain may simply not twist around enough ideas to make a good judgment.

Tax complexity is too much for even experienced investors comfortable with both mathematics and concepts. Mathematics has logic. Ideas tell a story. Tax complexity is complete nonsense. For example, the rules for withdrawal from tax-deferred retirement accounts are extremely difficult to understand. 401(k) tax complexity is beyond the comfort zone of most investors, yet few realize this.

Built-in resentment or regret

Investing has social costs as well as financial costs. Every period has its popular investments and its forgotten asset classes. Fashion changes, fads fade, and no one can keep up with all the latest hot new things. Inevitably, there will be regrets and resentments.

Even if you are in the right investment class, you might pick the wrong investment. Tech investors who bought IBM in 1988 regret they did not buy Microsoft instead. Real estate investors in the 1990s lost prestige to stock investors even though real estate returns for the decade were great. Their spouses and friends criticized them as out of touch. Cab drivers had stock tips for them. The investment magazines and newspapers dropped coverage of real estate and added tech stock sections.

Sometimes pressure comes from employers or family members to own certain investments or investment classes despite your own preference. Company stock is pushed on employees regardless of the prospects. Family real estate is to be held for generations even if poorly located and badly managed. Resentment is inevitable.

Some products are sold with great sales pressure. Annuities are foisted on unsuspecting buyers as safe, high return, and tax smart. In fact, they are low return, unstable, tax dumb, and very costly. The annuity buyer will eventually figure all this out and have regrets and resentments.

Many investors avoid resentments and regrets by never checking their results or by refusing to sell losers. Hoping to get even, they instead experience free-floating fears and anxieties.

Free-floating fear

Investment return comes from income and appreciation. A dividend check every quarter goes a long way toward eliminating fear. Investments that have no income and only appreciation or depreciation often lead to a sense of free-floating fear. Initial public offerings (IPOs) with no earnings or dividends, yet spending all their cash, create a sense of free-floating fear. Other investments have the same effect. Land pays no dividend. It just sits there waiting for an offer or development. Thoughts of toxic waste, zoning changes, polluting neighbors, and higher taxes are all manifestations of free-floating fears.

All investments expected to have high future returns create free-floating fear. The myth that long-term investors have nothing to fear from market declines leads to fear.

Any investment that has a history of extreme volatility also comes attached with free-floating fears. Commodities are especially volatile. The price of wheat can double or be cut in half in a month based on unpredictable weather patterns and overseas demand. Oil is subject to the whims of Oil Producing and Exporting Countries (OPEC) and environmentalists. In 1998, the price was $25 per barrel; in 1999, $10; in 2000, $35. Options combine volatility and an exercise deadline, forcing fear levels to rise as time compresses.

Many sources of the free-floating fears are subtle. Most investors are not aware of them. Savers cannot understand why they have fears with all their money in municipal bonds. They are in denial about how inflation slowly erodes purchasing power, turning seemingly profitable investments into losers. Bond fund investors get that odd feeling in their stomach even though they are in well-managed bond funds. Buried deep in the prospectus is that expense ratio that explains why the managers will make a killing even if the investors lose their nest egg.

Some people are more comfortable with free-floating fear than others. If it is troublesome for you, take a look at investments that are less likely to trigger free-floating fear.

People pleasing

Investing triggers all our character flaws. People pleasers have trouble with many investment scenarios. People pleasing is conforming to another person's will at the expense of our own self-interest. We feel if we say no to their requests, they will not like us or will not respect us as investors.

Profits are made in the sale of all investment products. Someone is always interested in getting you to buy. Stockbrokers want commissions, no-load mutual funds want expenses, banks want interest rate spreads on

CDs, Realtors want commissions. A people pleaser often buys investment products to make someone else happy and later finds himself miserable.

People other than salespeople can trigger people pleasing. Many people use their parents' broker to make their parents happy even if the broker turns out to be a stock churner. Even on discovering the truth, they continue to use the broker so their parents will not find out the broker is a crook and be alarmed. Employees commonly buy employer stock to please the boss even if the stock is a poor investment or renders their portfolio undiversified. During the tech bubble, many tech stocks were purchased to show other tech maniacs that you were part of the group.

Impulse buying

Irrational buying is not limited to people pleasing. Some investments are purchased on a mere impulse. No one is pleased, including the purchaser. An impulse is satisfied and that is all.

Before online trading, there were few investments that could trigger impulse buying. Today, any investment that can be bought and sold on the Internet is subject to impulse buying. Stocks and mutual funds are the most common impulse buys. Real estate requires weeks, if not months, and large cash outlays. Impulse buying is nearly impossible with real estate.

A pattern of impulse buying is a sign of self-destructive behavior. If you have made one or two impulse buys, look for investments in Chapter 4 that cannot be purchased online. If you can count more than 10 times when you have bought investments on impulse, you need additional help. Call a therapist.

Herd psychosis

Herd psychosis is a mass form of people pleasing. Members of the herd all conform to the seeming will of the herd, regardless of their individual self-interest. As the herd bids up prices, the chosen asset class soars in value. This draws more members into the herd and prices move beyond any measure of reasonable value. The size of the herd increases exponentially. Suddenly the herd sentiment switches to sell and then to panic. The vast majority of herd members come in late and suffer huge losses.

The total capitalization of an investment class determines its potential for herding. Large investment classes such as stocks and real estate have seen tremendous bubbles. Tax lien certificates, stamps, and other small asset classes have little herd potential.

Herd psychosis is not just the potential to be fashionable or trendy. All investments have periods of popularity. Oil and gas limited partnerships were hot from 1975–1984. However, they did not produce the herd instinct. The herd instinct is a feeling that you must invest in this asset class regardless of your economic circumstances or the prospects for the asset class. Although oil and gas limited partnerships were once very popular, few, if any, investors who could not afford the losses actually purchased interests.

The tech mania of 1996-2001 was an extreme example of herd psychosis. People with no savings borrowed on their credit cards to buy the hottest stocks. The phenomena was worldwide. Respected financial journalists recommended individual companies and advocated buying the dips. The gold and silver mania of the late-1970s was equally alluring. Investment advisors advocated 100-percent asset allocation to precious metals. Japanese real estate mania reached epic portions in 1989. A single property in Tokyo was worth more than all of Manhattan. The Tokyo crash and price adjustment continues more than 13 years later.

Those of you who find you have been sucked into more than one bubble, consider investments that are not prone to herd psychosis. If you find yourself always in bubbles and crashes, addiction is a possibility.

Addiction

The desire to make money from savings, investing, and speculating is natural. Increasing stock prices are attractive; compound interest is fascinating; rising rents put a smile on the landlord's face. It is only when the natural desire to make money investing exceeds normal bounds that addiction takes over. Greed is an extreme emotion. Few investors ever feel greed. The cliché that greed and fear are the only two emotions investors' feel is false. Greed is rare. Greed leads to extreme actions.

In the late 1990s, the lure of quick and easy profits caused many people to leave their jobs and trade stocks all day. With a small stake and a second mortgage, a credit line, a margin brokerage account, or several credit cards, greed led many on the path of addiction. The gold rush of 1849, the real estate boom of the early 1980s, and all other manias had similar results on a small band of investors. At the cost of losing work, homes, families, friends, and social standing, these lonely individuals pursued their greed.

Addiction includes large numbers in bubble periods. But it is always present and no class of investors is immune. Professional investors and money managers, as well as amateurs, are subject to addiction. A small group of professional traders and money managers became addicted to the tech trading mania as did a small group of individual investors.

Addiction is blinding. The addict, once addicted, does not see the costs. The addict knows on some level that with every trade there are commissions, spreads, and taxes to pay and that every loan has interest, fees, and a repayment schedule. All this is ignored for the desperately certain belief that a few great trades will lead to wealth. But wealth, even if achieved, does not fill the addict's need and is inevitably traded away.

Comfort zone emotions

Once you have found your comfort zone, you will experience few of these troubling emotions. A good night's sleep will be the norm. You will wake with enthusiasm for investing. After you have done your research or determined that there is nothing to do, you will feel a sense of satisfaction and well-being. Fear of financial insecurity will leave you, as will fear of financial professionals and institutions. You will no longer be sold inappropriate investments. You will no longer regret the mistakes you have made, but appreciate the lessons they have taught you. You will intuitively know how to approach new investments and consistently make good decisions to buy, sell, and avoid. Investing will be a confident area in your life. Though market crashes and events outside the norm will shake you at first, your recovery will be quick and your response positive. From every event, you will grow and mature as an investor and as a person. You will see how you can help others with their investment issues. You will derive a sense of meaning and satisfaction from helping others invest and from your own investment activities.

Look for your personality

This chapter is the start of the path toward your comfort zone. You may already recognize some of the causes of the roller coaster ride you have experienced from investing. The next chapters detail the emotional triggers in individual investments. Pay attention to investments you have owned or currently own. Ask if you have had the experience described. Then look for investments that may better fit your personality.

Your feelings are the road map to your comfort zone. Each feeling you have experienced tells you if a given investment is in or out of your comfort zone. Learn to ignore any advice you have heard that insists you must invest without emotion. You must let yourself experience all your feelings if you are to find your comfort zone. Without emotion, you are lost and subject to the sales pitch of a million investment hawkers.

CHAPTER 4

SAVINGS

*T*his chapter will help you consider how you react to savings instruments such as CDs and annuities. Also, it will show you to what degree you are a saver, an investor, or a speculator. Emotional traps are embedded in us, as well as in investment products. Internal traps come from our nature as savers, investors, and speculators. Everyone has an internal saver, investor, and speculator. However, everyone has different comfort levels with each aspect of his or her investment personality. When you hand money to a broker, you need to know which part of you is opening your fist.

Not all readers need to study this chapter. After reading the following section, you might wish to look only at the sections on savings instruments you now own or have owned in the past. Then, those of you who have a strong sense that you are a saver should study the entire chapter. Those who are confident that savings instruments are not within your comfort zone should skip the rest of the chapter. If you are not sure, skim the rest of the chapter.

Saving as faith

Saving is as old as humankind. Ancient tribes stored grain, seeds, implements, and ceremonial objects. Anthropological digs unearth bins and storage jars filled with valuable treasures.

The emotions associated with savings are deeply ingrained in our psyche. Saving requires work beyond producing the daily bread. Hard work creates a sense of entitlement. Workers earn their Social Security payments. Savings are not a gift from anyone. Savers do not trust individuals with their hard-earned cash. Only God or good government can be trusted.

Saving requires a deep faith that the excess will be preserved for future use. A safe community is necessary; without it, savings will be stolen. Saving tests our faith in the community.

Today we save as a community through government-guaranteed bank accounts, Social Security taxes, and other government taxes and programs. The current debate over Social Security and Medicare is part of our ritual and ceremony. A threat to savings is a threat to the whole community. The idea that Social Security should be "invested" in stocks challenges the sacred nature of savings.

Savings evoke deep emotions. Saving is about entitlement and faith, not fear and greed. Entitlement and faith are derived from generational experience, religion, and the meaning of life. Every community has had a Great Depression. Hard work does not always produce excess. When the well runs dry, the community ends. Communities such as the Inca and the Anasazi tribes worked hard, created vast roads and irrigation system, yet disappeared from the planet. Hard work does not guarantee anything. The Roaring 20s were full of frivolity, yet produced abundance; the 30s witnessed hard labor that did not overcome scarcity.

Good gods or good government are required to produce savings. The ancient tribes had rituals, harvest festivals, and the like to protect and celebrate their savings. Their feelings were primal and intense: gratitude for the bounty of nature but entitlement to share that bounty once harvested and stored. Every member of the tribe was involved. Today, feelings about savings are just as primal and intense, and involve every member of society.

When savings systems collapse, no one is unaffected. In the 1930s, massive bank failures lead to deflation in some countries and hyperinflation in others. Incredibly strong feelings were unleashed. Desperation led to Nazism, wars, revolutions, and massive New Deals. When all savings disappear, gods are abandoned and governments overthrown.

All forms of savings entail a sense of trust and entitlement. This is widely recognized. A dollar in savings must always be worth a dollar. Though savings instruments pay interest, the inflexible value of the principal is of primary importance. The main short-term savings instruments are passbook savings accounts, CDs, and money market funds. Long-term savings instruments include government notes and bonds. Many people also consider their primary residence as a savings instrument.

Savings accounts, CDs, and money market funds

Though savings trigger intense emotions, trigger events for the intense emotions are rare. In addition, the number of emotions triggered by savings accounts, CDs, and money market funds is small. Short-term savings investments are sold as security. If you need predictability, these are the investments for you. One dollar invested here should always be worth $1, never 99 cents.

The purchase of CDs and money market funds can lead to some confusion and complexity. CDs have different interest rates and different maturities. Unpredictable forces including the Federal Reserve, the economy, and inflation determine the interest rate on CDs, money market funds, and savings accounts.

Money market funds compete based on different interest rates, and interest rates fluctuate daily. Professional money managers who charge varying expenses run money market funds. At times, the fund sponsor, as a promotional gimmick, defers these expenses. There are also several types of money market funds, such as treasury funds, municipal funds, and commercial paper funds. However, compared to most investments, the purchase of short-term securities is relatively simple.

Ideally, during the time you own short-term securities you will have only a sense of confidence that your dollar is always worth a dollar and your interest, however small, is always accumulating. When this confidence is threatened, expect powerful emotions including a sense of betrayal and a loss of faith. When the dollar value of the principal is threatened, savers take to the streets and to the polls to preserve that value. The FSLIC (Federal Savings and Loan Insurance Corporation) and the FDIC (Federal Deposit Insurance Corporation) guaranteed savings and loan (S&L) and bank savings instruments for up to $100,000. The savings and loan crisis of the early 1990s created a scare that these guarantees would not be honored; failed banks and S&Ls might redeem CDs and savings accounts at less than face value. In the 1980s, the S&L industry made contributions to politicians in order to secure deregulation of the industry. Thereafter, they were able to invest federally insured funds in risky enterprises. When the enterprises failed and the S&Ls were unable to pay back federally insured depositors, the indebted politicians began to argue that the federal guarantees should not be honored. Savers should have evaluated the trustworthiness of banks and S&Ls before they saved with them. Emotions became extreme. Politicians were booted out of office; Charles Keating and other bank officers were prosecuted for criminal offenses; and the guarantee to savings was retained. From this, money market fund sponsors learned that the principal value of the fund could not fluctuate even in the worst economic crisis or savers would only place money in federally insured products.

Money market funds are not government guaranteed. Betrayal is a slight risk with money market funds. In rare instances, the dollar value gets broken. Money market funds are a collection of the highest-rated, 90-day, commercial debt and government paper. By law, money market funds must have 95 percent of their assets in top-rated debt. Still, defaults occur. The highest-rated companies can suddenly fall apart. Enron is a recent example. When the bankruptcy of a 90-day debt issuer threatens the dollar value of money market accounts, fund sponsors routinely add cash from their own pockets to cover the loss. A large fund sponsor sells stocks, bonds, mutual funds, and other lucrative securities. The cost in bad publicity from a money market fund loss would be immense. Though you may feel threatened by the bankruptcy of a 90-day debt issuer that the value of your money market funds will decline, there is little chance it will take place.

Because money market funds do not have FDIC or other insurance, there have been rare cases of fraud where investor money was stolen. Money market funds pay higher interest than most FDIC-insured products. Consider whether or not this higher interest is worth taking a very small risk. The risks of fraud are small, but any risk may be outside your comfort zone.

The biggest issues with money market funds involve impulse buying of stuff you do not need and becoming a target for sales pitches from the sales force that sold you the money market fund. Money market funds can be tapped with checks, credit cards, and online transfers. Impulse buyers may want to avoid the opportunity to make quick purchases. Some brokers who are slightly unscrupulous tell money market fund owners that they should "put their money to work" and that "cash is trash." Lured by potentially higher returns in stocks and other high-commission, high-spread investments, money market funds are easily and quickly converted. With CDs, you lose your interest if you liquidate before the term. Savings accounts often require several steps to convert into risky investments. Money market funds, particularly those attached to brokerage accounts, can be converted at the click of a mouse. If you are vulnerable to sales pitches or impulse buying, you may not want to own money market funds.

During ownership, some savers also experience a sense of regret. High inflation in the 1970s reduced the purchasing power of savings and was not compensated for by interest paid. When real estate was hot in the early 1980s, savers regretted they were not participating. The stock bubble of the late 1990s also led to regrets and jealousy. However, savers who hold out experience a sense of satisfaction when bubbles burst and speculators scramble to place their remaining funds in savings instruments.

When CDs mature and must be rolled over, savers experience a mixed set of emotions. Higher interest rates can lead to joy unless inflation has risen such that purchasing power will be lost. Lower rates can lead to regret that a long-term investment was not made.

Liquidating savings often triggers many emotions. A source of security is dying. When savings must be substantially liquidated, a grieving process begins. The saver may experience a wide range of emotions including sadness, regret, anger, resentment, helplessness, confusion, and free-floating fear. Generally, the cause of liquidation will compound the emotional mix. A divorce often requires a non-working spouse to both watch her savings dwindle as she reenters the work force and grieves the loss of her marriage.

U. S. government notes and bonds

The range of emotion from government notes and bonds is similar to that for short-term securities. While many may be asking why corporate notes and bonds are not included here, the answer is simple. Corporate debt is risky. Only investors and speculators should consider it. U.S. government notes and bonds are for savers whose primary concern is the return of their principal and whose secondary concern is the receipt of interest. There is a real possibility of losing some principal with corporate debt.

Before purchasing treasuries, you will be exposed to complexity. The possibilities in government bonds are great. You can invest for one year or 29 years or any period in between. Certain bonds, such as Series EE, H, and I have tax advantages. Interest rates differ for every maturity and every type of bond. For most notes and bonds, the principal value is fixed. For inflation-indexed treasuries, known as TIPs, the principal value increases every year we experience inflation. The principal value of I bonds also adjusts with inflation. However, even though the principal value of most bonds or notes is fixed, bonds sell at prices higher or lower than the principal value, depending on the current level of interest rates and the supply and demand of similar bonds and notes. The mathematics of computing the proper price for a note or bond is complex.

The complexity of purchase may lead you to rely on a salesperson. Government bonds are purchased from brokers, banks, and directly from the federal government. Buying from brokers and banks can bring up issues of trust. Whereas you may have a great degree of confidence that government bonds are secure and the tax consequences predictable, you may not trust that the product you are being sold benefits you as much as it benefits the salesperson. Buying treasuries directly from the federal government might also create fear. You may believe that with a salesperson holding your hand, you would find a better product at a better price.

Government notes and bonds are often sold in bundles as managed mutual funds, unmanaged index funds and trusts, or as closed-end mutual funds. Here the issues get more complex. Built-in resentment and regret are inevitable. Fees and commissions must be paid to mutual fund managers, brokers, and closed-end fund managers. These funds rarely do better than notes and bonds bought by an individual and held to maturity. It is easy to regret the fees paid for poorly performed services. Yet some savers feel the need to use professionals to pick bonds for them. They would have free-floating fear and worry if they were to construct a portfolio of bonds on their own. You must ask yourself how you are likely to react.

Often, managed funds turn out to be different than expected. Savers primarily want their principal returned when a note or bond matures. Some funds are managed without regard to principal fluctuations. Many savers have found the government fund they purchased paid out both principal and interest so that at the end there was no principal left. Alternatively, the manager of the fund borrowed extensively to juice the returns from the fund and instead lost a substantial portion of the principal. You are likely to feel betrayed if you unwittingly purchased a fund with fluctuating principal values.

Bond investors often experience regret and resentment when other asset classes have dramatic rises. Longer duration bonds cause the most distress. Savers who put money into 30-year Treasuries in 1994 received annual yields up to 8 percent. They had to stand by and watch as stocks returned better than 20 percent a year for the next five years. However, the dramatic decline in 2000-2001 may have given them some satisfaction.

Volatility is an issue with notes and bonds that mature in two or more years. Before OPEC, floating interest rates, interest rate swaps, floating exchange rates, budget surpluses, and electronic trading, treasury bonds had low volatility. Today, Treasuries can lose 20 percent of their value in a month. Savers waiting for bonds to mature will feel fear when they learn of the current value of their holdings. They must be able to process the fear and wait to maturity. Savers who cash out may have regrets and resentments when bond prices turn up again.

Occasionally, bond investors experience complete powerlessness. When interest rates and inflation rise dramatically, the value of bonds declines dramatically. If prospects are for continued high interest rates and inflation, bond interest will never compensate for lost purchasing power. In the 1960s, government bonds paid 5 percent or less in interest. During the 1970s, inflation averaged better than 8 percent. Bond investors who bought in the 1960s sat by powerless as the purchasing power of their principal and interest dwindled.

On the other hand, treasuries are the best asset class during extended periods of deflation. In the 1930s, treasury savers had to guard against grandiosity rather than inferiority. Treasuries were the best asset class.

Selling government bonds before maturity brings up feelings of regret if interest rates have risen and the bonds must be sold for less than face value. Commissions, as well as spreads, must also be paid.

Letting bonds mature eliminates both commissions and spreads. Still, when bonds mature, the saver is faced with the dilemma of what to do with the principal. For some, the answer is simple. Others experience anxiety. Savers who fret over what to buy may be more comfortable in bond funds where the money manager makes all the buy decisions.

Municipal bonds

Unmanageability is a big issue with municipal bonds (munis). (Munis are bonds issued by states and local governments.) State and local government bonds are less secure than federal government bonds. The federal government can print money to pay bond interest and principal. With munis, defaults are possible, because state and local governments do not have the power to print money. Although defaults are rare, they occur. Many munis are secured by specific projects. If the project is bad, the muni could default. Other munis are secured by a general fund. However, mismanagement of the general fund can endanger your muni. For example, the Orange County (California) general fund in 1993 and 1994 was run like a hedge fund. The fund manager invested in derivatives and leveraged up the fund just when interest rates rose dramatically, bankrupting the county. This type of mismanagement can lead to feelings of outrage among bondholders.

Munis are sometimes insured, but the insurer needs to be solid for the insurance to be any help. State and local governments sometimes establish a fund, known as a sinking fund, to be used to pay off specific bonds when they come due. These bonds are known as prefunded bonds. Prefunded bonds are more secure as long as the sinking fund is never attached.

Municipal bonds also have call provisions that allow the issuer to redeem bonds before their term expires. For example, a 30-year bond will typically have a seven-year call. If interest rates have declined over the seven-year period, the state will redeem the bonds and then issue lower-yielding securities. Obviously, this is not in your favor, and you may find it irritating.

Munis are also subject to wide swings in value. State economies are more volatile than the national economy. When a state economy is booming, state tax revenues are high and there is little need to issue munis. At the same time, state residents' incomes are high. They want munis, which pay tax-free interest. The combination of low supply and high demand leads to overpriced, scarce bonds. When a state is in recession, tax revenues decline. The state issues a hoard of bonds to keep going just at the time when it can least afford to make interest and principal payments. Muni interest rates rise to compensate for the reduced security. Older munis lose value. Consider how you react to wide price swings.

Munis have tremendous tax advantages. Interest paid is not subject to federal, state, or local taxes. However, many savers will find the tax advantage caused them to invest outside their comfort zone. Calls, volatility, and insecure principal may be more than you can handle.

Trust issues are worse for muni funds than for other bond funds. Muni funds offer the advantage of diversification and professional management. Unfortunately, the fees eat up as much as 25 percent of your interest. This is seldom worthwhile. Muni fund managers rarely outperform a list of unmanaged bonds. Many also try to rev up returns with lower credit issues, including junk munis, and borrow against the fund to increase investments in an attempt to time the market. These tactics are not likely to improve your sleep.

Muni funds can also play with the value of your shares to your disadvantage. Muni issues are rarely traded. Muni managers can use any reasonable value for fund assets. Though credit quality may have deteriorated, managers often refrain from writing down asset values for fear of losing shareholders. However, at some point asset values must be marked to market to avoid outright fraud and jail time for the fund managers. If you buy fund shares at a high valuation of assets and later have to redeem when assets are written down to realistic levels, you will justifiably feel betrayed.

Fund managers can also turn tax-free munis into taxable bonds. Capital gains from selling appreciated muni bonds are taxable. Individual savers typically hold munis until maturity so there are no capital gains. Muni fund managers trade bonds. This creates capital gains, often short-term capital gains, which are taxed at the highest rate. Muni funds are outside the comfort zone of most savers.

Insurance products

Insurance companies sell many products to savers. Unfortunately, all of these products are less safe than CDs, money market funds, and treasury obligations. Even worse, some of these products are certain to deplete your capital. Few insurance products are within a pure saver's comfort zone.

Guaranteed Investment Contracts (GICs)

The safety of principal in some saving instruments is illusory. Guaranteed investment contracts (GICs) are short-term savings instruments available in 401(k) plans. Participating GICs pay variable interest; non-participating GICs pay fixed interest. GICs are issued by insurance companies. The insurance company guarantees the interest rate for the term of the contract. Unfortunately, in both varieties, the dollar value of principal is not guaranteed. The value of principal is only as good as the insurance company. A busted GIC will lead to resentments, regrets, anger, and even rage.

Insurance companies compete to sell GICs to 401(k) plans. These are very lucrative products for insurers. In order to increase sales, they pump up the interest rate by investing in junk bonds and other high-interest, high-risk securities. Be aware that high-yield GICs may guarantee interest, but principal is at stake. If the insurance company goes bankrupt, GIC owners get paid after policyholders, and policyholders rarely get all their money unless states insure them. No one insures GIC owners.

Savers are under the illusion that 401(k)s and the saving products they offer are safe. Remember that these are not FDIC-insured plans and they do not offer FDIC-insured products.

Also be aware that 401(k) plan sponsors are making money from these plans and the products create fees for insurance companies, mutual fund companies, and financial planners. You are paying all those fees whether you are aware of it or not. Disillusionment is a real possibility with GICs.

The enticement to buy a GIC is a tax deduction for funding a 401(k). Be aware that a tax deduction may induce you to save outside your comfort zone. True savers may be happier without the tax deduction and with an FDIC guarantee.

Annuities

Retirement savers want a secure source of income during retirement. Annuities are investments that pay a fixed sum every month for a fixed period, often the investor's lifetime or a spouse's lifetime. Most annuities also require a purchase of life insurance. Annuities are fine as long as you do not know what you are doing. Once you know what you are doing, you will experience regret if you have purchased an annuity.

Most fee-based investment advisors, as well as many industry magazines, advise against the purchase of annuities. There are many reasons for this.

Annuities are sold through aggressive sales techniques. If you have a problem with pleasing others to your own detriment, stay away from insurance salespeople. Some unscrupulous annuity salespeople prey on your fears of financial insecurity, confuse you with the complexity of investing for retirement, distort the tax aspects of annuities, and fail to disclose the huge commission they will receive out of your annuity purchase. Commissions of 8 percent are normal for annuities; this loss of 8 percent of your capital is very detrimental for true savers. True savers' primary concern is preservation of capital.

Complexity may lead you to purchase a product you do not need. Annuities combine life insurance and an investment product. Many investors seeking one or the other end up with both, though often neither fit their needs.

Once you have purchased an annuity, disappointment will follow. Some insurance companies are poor investors. Combine this with high expenses, and you get low returns on your annuities. An annuity that invests entirely in bonds will pay you as little as half the return you could receive owning bonds outright. An annuity invested in stocks will always underperform the stock market due to the loss of capital paid out as commissions on purchase and the annual high expenses.

Salespeople may take advantage of your disappointment. They will offer to exchange your poor performer tax-free for another annuity. If you take the bait, it will cost you another 8 percent of your capital in commissions as well as other charges.

Annuities have other negative surprises for you. Annuities are not liquid. If you need your money before retirement, you cash out at a loss because you are forced to pay a surrender charge. Surrender charges can be as high as 12 percent of your capital and they are due on exchanges as well as on a cash-out.

Annuities are also tax disadvantaged. Contributions are not tax deductible, but withdrawals of earnings are taxed at the highest tax rates.

Your greed can hurt you with annuities. Though contributions are not deductible, there are no limits on the amount of money you can contribute to annuities and earning on annuities are tax-deferred until you withdraw funds. There are limits on the amount of contributions to IRAs, 401(k)s, and other tax-deferred plans. Seeking solely to avoid taxes on the investment profits before withdrawal, many savers place large sums of money in annuities. Unfortunately, high expenses, poor returns, surrender charges, and the highest tax rates on withdrawal result in much worse performance than simply saving in Treasury bonds or CDs.

The annuity purchase could lead to hopelessness. If you have most of your retirement money in annuities and the insurance company goes bankrupt, you will not be able to retire. Annuities do not have FDIC insurance, and most states do not insure annuities. Annuities are only as good as the insurance company. Poor investment skills combined with high salaries, bonuses, and benefits have bankrupted many insurance companies.

Few savers will be happy with annuities once they understand what they have purchased.

Whole life

Whole life insurance plans can be equally troubling for savers. Whole life and universal life plans combine a bond portfolio with life insurance. Each premium pays partially for the insurance and partially to build up the bond portfolio.

You must be able to make regular monthly payments to be happy with these plans. A missed payment in the early years will terminate the life coverage and cost you part or all of your equity. You may find it easy to make a mortgage payment or pay rent each month because failure to do so renders you homeless. However, making a voluntary contribution to savings each month is another matter. Those of you who lack the ability to make regular, voluntary payments will be happier with CDs and savings accounts that can be funded at your discretion.

People pleasing is an issue with these policies. Some insurance sales-people will show you slick brochures and charts promising that after 10 to 15 years, interest on the bond portfolio will exceed the insurance premium. Thereafter, no further premium need be paid. Then you can use excess bond interest to either increase insurance coverage or increase the size of the bond portfolio. If you buy the sales pitch, resentments and regrets will follow.

Eventually, you will have to accept the fact that some insurers are lousy bond investors and charge high fees to manage the bond portfolios. These fees come out of your interest. Premiums will not vanish as quickly as promised. In fact, you may be paying premiums twice as long or longer than you anticipated.

Insurance salespeople will offer you a solution. They will be happy to put you into variable life. Variable life invests in stocks, not bonds. They will claim that higher returns from variable life will get you to a premium-free position faster. Before you purchase, ask about the commissions they re-ceive, the record the company has investing in stocks, and the fact that stocks pay no interest and can decline in value for 15 years. After you have heard their answers, consider whether, as a saver, a variable life plan is outside your comfort zone.

Whole life insurance is also hard to get rid of once you commit. You will have to pay surrender charges and will not get back all the commissions you paid. Once the policy is self-sustaining, you can withdraw your interest in excess of that needed to sustain the premiums, but that won't be much money. You can also sell the policy to a third party, but they will pay you far less than it is worth. Few savers are comfortable with whole life plans. A combination of CDs or Treasury bonds and term insurance is more likely within your comfort zone.

The saver personality

Though there are emotional quirks with true saving instruments, the frequency of trauma is low. Saving instruments are for investors who value predictability and are not troubled by jealousy, resentment, or regret when other investments produce spectacular returns and make headlines. Long-term returns on savings instruments are lower than for other investment classes. For those who value peace of mind, the price of lost returns is more than reasonable.

Savings instruments are also good for investors who do not want to spend time on their investments. Buy and ignore is a good philosophy for savers. Someone who needs to be out of the country for five years should leave her money in savings instruments. Blind neglect is often advocated for stocks, but in fact, there are too many five-year periods when stocks lose half their value.

Picking Treasury bonds requires a few hours each year. Higher yields can be found in agency issues and older bonds. Call provisions must be evaluated. The time requirements are minimal.

Investors looking for action should look elsewhere. If you enjoy lots of research, or want to interact with people such as tenants, other investors, or money managers, savings instruments are not for you. While you can create excitement trading bonds, you cannot create profits. High-energy investors should stay clear. Disappointment will follow.

Treasury bonds are also the only insurance against deflation. Savers who worry that current Japanese deflation may be exported to the United States or that there will be a return to deflation of the 1930s will feel safe here. Savers concerned with inflation will be comfortable with TIPs and money market funds.

The family home

Most Americans have the majority of their savings tied up in their home. Beyond making a mortgage payment, few savers are able to put away excess income. The government encourages saving in homes. Mortgage interest is tax-deductible. Credit card interest is not. Profit on the sale of a residence is tax-exempt up to $500,000. Government programs support first-time buyers and lower interest rates for low-income homeowners.

Realtors play up the savings aspect of homeownership. Savers are shown charts of home appreciation and tax savings compared to renters. This leads to overconfidence. Despite government support, a family home is an erratic savings vehicle.

The value of a dollar invested in a family home is not fixed. Home equity can swing up and down. When the local economy is bad, homeowners who lose their jobs often find out that they have lost all the savings in their home as well. In the late 1980s, the oil belt recession forced a massive loss of both jobs and homes. In the early 1990s, New England had a similar episode caused by the collapse of the real estate industry. The massive closing of military bases and defense plants a few years later caused thousands of Southern California residents to lose both jobs and homes. When a home is worth less than the mortgage, even employed homeowners have lost all their savings.

In a growing economy, equity can still be threatened. Home equity does not deserve the same confidence as FDIC insured CDs. Neighborhoods can change, hurting home values. Residential neighborhoods become commercial, family neighborhoods get drug infested, single family homes are cut up and become multifamily units eliminating all the parking and reducing values. Soon there will be a massive exodus from family neighborhoods as baby boomers retire and move to retirement communities.

Interest rate changes also threaten home equity. Higher mortgage rates make homes less affordable, which hurts home values. When homeowners hear or read about the Federal Reserve, most wonder how this will affect the value of their home. Higher real estate taxes also hurt home values.

Home equity is often disappointing as a savings vehicle. It lacks the utility of other savings systems. Unmanageability is a common occurrence. Just when you need your savings the most, home equity is likely to fail you. Laid-off workers often find they cannot tap their home equity with a second mortgage or refinance because they have no income to support higher mortgage payments. Retirees are often disappointed to find that the sale of their home after Realtor commissions and expenses leaves a much smaller nest egg than hoped for. Reverse mortgages often produce insufficient income for retiree living expenses. Savers relying on home equity must be prepared for sadness and grieving if their retirement plans are unreachable.

Home equity is also subject to herding instinct. In the oil belt from 1975–1983, money flowed out of the stock market and into homes. Seeking to get in on the mania, savers used all their savings as down payments and took on mortgages that they could not afford, expecting ever-rising home equity to allow them to get out at a profit. Prices reached unsustainable levels. When the price of oil collapsed, so did the price of homes. Massive amounts of savings were destroyed. New York has had similar episodes of condo fever caused by the rise and fall of Wall Street. California has always been subject to hysteria around home prices. Silicon Valley home equity is as volatile as tech stocks.

The biggest treat to home equity is impulse buying and keeping up appearances in a consumer society. Have you taken out a second mortgage even though you consider home equity your retirement nest egg? Many people run up credit card debt and then refinance it at a lower rate with a second mortgage. At some point, though, the nest egg disappears. Impulse buying and keeping up appearances can turn savers into spendthrifts.

Still, there is some justification for using a home as a savings vehicle. We all need to have a residence. The purpose of saving is to create a sense of financial security in our lives. Renters are subject to rent increases and the whims of landlords. A long-term saver able to pay a mortgage and not take out second and third mortgages will not have rent increases. A long-term saver able to pay off the mortgage will dramatically increase the sense of financial security in his life. Investors and speculators will have little interest in this type of security.

Home ownership works best for long-term savers who are not interested in the value of their home, but the security of their lifestyle. They are able to ignore the ups and downs of home prices, interest rates, and the economy, and focus on paying down the mortgage one payment at a time. Often, true savers double their mortgage payments to eliminate the mortgage at a faster, orderly pace, whereas investors would not dream of using their excess cash to increase a mortgage payment.

CHAPTER 5

THINK TWICE, FEEL TWICE, BEFORE YOU INVEST

*I*nvesting triggers different emotions than saving. As you read this chapter, determine if you are more comfortable with investment emotions than with savings emotions. There is a wide range of investments. Given your current state of self-knowledge, also consider which specific investments might be within your comfort zone and which might not. When you reach Step 3, you will use these insights to match your personality to investments.

Not all readers need to study this chapter. After reading the following section, you might want to look only at the sections on investments you now own or have owned in the past. Those of you who have a strong sense that you are an investor should study the entire chapter. Those who are confident that investments are not within your comfort zone should skip the rest of the chapter. If you are not sure, skim the rest of the chapter.

Are you an investor?

Investors are ambitious and optimistic. Unlike humble savers, they believe that taking a little risk and exerting a minimal effort will dramatically increase their funds.

Investing can be very troubling, but it touches fewer core emotions than savings. When ambition is thwarted and optimism is shattered, investors are miserable. However, they do not storm the capital and start a revolution.

Investing concerns one-on-one relationships rather than the role of God and society in safeguarding hard-earned money. Whereas savers trust no one individual, optimistic investors trust too many people. When markets collapse, individuals are blamed, not government or the gods.

Ideally, the investor only invests excess savings. In investing, an individual or a group lends their excess savings to other individuals or groups for a fee. The fee is rent, interest, dividends, or capital appreciation. Groups can be corporations, partnerships, trusts, or other legal entities. The investor relies on the investee to pay the fee over time and to repay the investment. Investing creates a relationship between the investor and the investee. Each has expectations of the other. Emotions are triggered entering the relationship, during the relationship, and leaving the relationship.

Investing involves small segments of society: businesses, individual farms, buildings, and entrepreneurs. Only recently, with the advent of index funds, has investing concerned the whole of a large market: the stock market. Index funds are mutual funds that buy shares in every stock in a given segment of the market. Buying index funds, you can buy a piece of the whole stock market. Still, the stock market is only one segment of society, though currently a large segment.

The investor trusts the investee. When this trust is broken, strong emotions are unleashed. Utility stockholders are furious when a utility cuts or eliminates its dividend. When a tenant defaults on a lease and forces a property into foreclosure, the property owner has a wide range of emotions triggered by the breach of trust. Some vow never to own real estate again.

Sometimes the investment exceeds expectations. Wal-Mart investors saw their small regional chain become the largest retailer in the world. Berkshire Hathaway went from a shell company to one of the world's largest corporations. Success triggers grandiosity in some, frivolity in others. Many successful investors are disoriented and unhappy.

However, faith is also a part of investing. The borrower, tenant, or business owner believes the application of science and technology to business practices will produce more than the sum of capital and labor, thus enabling him to pay the rent, interest, dividends, or capital appreciation plus enough for his own savings. Productivity, technology, and efficiency are the creed of investors.

For savings to increase, the saver must take action. The ancient saver must go back to the field and grow more crops, harvest them, process them, and store them in bins. The investor simply relies on time, the actions of others, and the forces of productivity to increase values. Investors research investees to determine the likelihood of this magic transpiring. Investors expect high returns without their own labor. When this faith is unrequited, they are deeply disappointed. As Internet companies folded, investors were hurt both by financial losses and by the betrayal of faith in the unlimited productivity potential of the Web.

Investors also rely on society. Stable economic conditions are important for investors. Investing concerns the value of currency. Inflation, deflation, supply and demand: All are part of the investment scene. Ancient savers relied on the utility of the product saved, not the currency value of the paper interest in another's actions or productivity. However, investors' reactions to their relationship with their investees are much more powerful than their reactions to economic conditions.

For a fee, many parties facilitate the transfer of investment capital to investees. Stockbrokers, Realtors, bankers, money managers, mutual funds, newsletter writers, and other financial professionals siphon off pieces of investment capital. While investors seek to make high returns with little or no work, financial professionals seek to obtain high wages with little notice. This relationship is the source of many troubling emotions.

In 1980, real estate was the largest class of investments. Today, the value of stocks far exceeds the value of real estate. Many investors are wondering if they are compatible with stocks. Let's take a look at stocks first.

Stocks

Marketed as simple and easy to own, stocks are actually the most complex and emotionally challenging of all asset classes. Powerlessness, unmanageability, regrets, fears, social pressures, herd behavior, and complexities galore are the norm.

Stock investors are primarily an optimistic group. They believe that stocks they purchase will increase in value. They all know stories of stocks that increased in value by 100 times or more. The potential rewards appear unlimited. Of course, most stock investors are aware of the risk of loss, so they diversify and employ other cautions. Still, every stock investor believes that one or more of his stocks or mutual funds will have fantastic returns.

Businesses issuing stock encourage this belief and are all too happy to accept the investor's cash.

Do you have any business owning stocks?

At the micro level, a stock is an ownership interest in a business. The earnings from the business belong to the stockholders. Theoretically, the employees of the business, including top management, work for the stockholders. In practice, the employees are self-interested. Every employee, from the CEO to the janitorial crew, wants as large a piece of the earnings as possible, leaving as little for you as can be justified. You may have emotional difficulty with this built-in conflict of interest.

Elaborate schemes are routinely employed to siphon off your interests. In the old days, two-thirds of profits were paid out as dividends, giving you direct control of a large portion of earnings. Today, dividends are cut or eliminated so employees can use profits as they see fit. Fewer than half of today's stocks pay any dividends at all. Every year the number of dividend payers declines. Even those that pay dividends pay only token amounts. Instead, employees grant themselves raises and bonuses without consulting shareholders. Insider boards of directors grant themselves profit-sharing plans, stock, and stock options, all to your deficit. Board remuneration committees offer excessive pay for executives in exchange for excessive pay for themselves. The few profits that are left are often squandered on ill-advised acquisitions and other schemes. Hundreds of examples could be cited including the recent debacles at Enron, Lucent, Rite Aid, Millennium, Color Tile, Dow Chemical, Sunbeam, Trump Hotels & Casinos, Reliance Groups, and many Internet, tech, and telecom firms that crashed in 2000-2001.

Stock options are particularly troubling. In theory, employees who own stock will work to make the price of the stock rise. Therefore they are given the right to buy shares at a discount. Unfortunately, when new stock is issued to employees who exercise their stock options, your interest is diluted. In some companies, you will find your interest cut in half in a few years. CEOs of large companies average $4 million a year in stock options. In addition, studies show that the share prices of companies that issue large amounts of stock options underperform the market. Even worse, employees benefit when the stock price collapses. Stock options are repriced or new stock options issued so employees can dilute your interest at a fraction of the cost. You get no benefit from a stock price collapse.

The grant of stock options also increases the volatility of your shares. Stock options are only valuable if the price of the stock rises above the option price. If the value declines, the options are worthless, and employees will not spend money to exercise them. This gives employees an incentive to bet the company on risky ventures such as mergers, acquisitions, untested products, untested markets, untested technology, and untested corporate structures. Employee stock options are no benefit to you whatsoever.

Innumerable financial and accounting schemes, all legal, also dilute your share of profits. Accounting tricks include non-deducted stock options, accruing unearned sales and commissions, classifying big losses as non-deducted special items, and counting pension gains as income. All tricks make earnings appear higher than they really are. Creating huge reserves in a bad year is common as well. This allows the company to then post high earnings in succeeding years. Many companies also use cash flow to speculate in the stock of hot companies. This boosts profits quickly, though it turns a solid business into a volatile investment fund. Companies also finance purchases by shaky customers. This boosts sales and profits in the short-term but leads to huge write-offs later when the shaky customers fail.

All these accounting tricks inflate profits short-term. Higher profits justify higher salaries, bonuses, and grants of stock options. When these tricks are discovered and set right, earnings are restated and your stock price collapses. However, bonuses and salaries are long gone and stock options cashed. A series of legal accounting schemes can siphon off all earnings and leave the company bankrupt and you holding a worthless stock certificate. Enron is a recent example. Enron used off balance sheet entities to inflate profits and enrich management. When the tricks were discovered, the stock price collapsed; outside shareholders ended up with penny stocks.

Highly public maneuvers can dilute your interests as well. Bank loans are taken out and bonds are issued, taking control of the company away from you and granting it to bankers and the whims of the bond market. New shares issues are sold to the public, diluting your stake. Mergers and acquisitions of other companies further dilute your power and tighten the hold of management over your earnings.

Investor relations departments are set up to divert your attention from what is really going on and to placate your reaction. Companies often buy back their own shares, indicating that this will increase your ownership interest. What is really going on is that your interest is transferred elsewhere. Bought-back shares are placed in employee stock ownership plans or financed by bonds and bank loans. When it is all over, employees and lenders own more of the company and you own less.

Ask yourself: How does all this makes me feel? You may feel betrayed or abandoned. Your broker or financial planner never mentioned the fact that simply buying stock is likely to make a sucker out of you. Certainly, a sense of unmanageability begins at this level.

I want to point out that difficulties with employees is not going to change. The interests of shareholders and employees have always been and always will be opposed. In fact, in the last two decades, employees have increasingly siphoned off a larger and larger share of profits. According to a 2001 study by Sanford C. Bernstein & Co., accounting tricks disguised the fact that there was no growth in profits between 1995 and 2001. Nevertheless, salaries, bonuses, and stock options soared. Industries in which shareholders have no chance to make a profit may soon be the norm. Claims that stocks are the best investment for the long-run ignore this trend.

You cannot change the fact that employees have an advantage over shareholders. This is an inalterable, long-term fact of stock investing. You must focus on yourself, not them. If you can handle a long-term relationship with decades of built-in conflict, stocks may be for you. If you currently have great difficulty with conflict in relationships, yet you really want to own stocks, you may be able to change. Always ask how you can change, not how you can change them, or how they can change themselves. However, be realistic about how much emotional turmoil you can handle and how much you will have to change internally if you are going to stay in stocks. Even if you can handle the conflict of interest with employees, there are other equally difficult issues.

How swiftly can you process your emotions?

Stocks trade on exchanges. Because dividends are either small or non-existent, the value of your stock is determined solely by what other investors are willing to pay for it. In a calm market, you will experience a sense of unmanageability, because there is nothing you can do to force others to raise the price of your stocks. Even small losses in calm markets can be troubling because investors rarely want to admit their mistakes, feel the pain of loss, and move on. Focusing on prices rather than the cause of the losses, they hang on to losers until they can break even.

Optimism can grow into fantasy. Investors sometimes fall in love with their companies. They fantasize about new products and skyrocketing stock prices. All evidence of deteriorating fundamentals is rationalized away or ignored. Individual stocks can decline for years or decades. Believing fantasy can lead to many years of pain even in calm markets. However, we have seen few calm markets in recent years, and volatile markets are more troublesome.

In most markets, stock losses happen quickly. A bad earnings report can cut a stock price in half. An unexpected rate hike by the federal government can knock the whole market down 15 percent in a month. For still unexplained reasons, the whole market dropped 22 percent on October 19, 1987. Few investments move so quickly. Real estate rarely moves 1 percent a month. Unless you can process your emotions quickly, stocks will cause you a lot of pain.

Stock prices will always be volatile. Every form of media extensively covers the stock market. As a result, stock prices are influenced by all major events, whether they are political, social, or economic. Elections, earthquakes, terrorists, unemployment, assassinations, foreign affairs, the dollar, war, peace, and much more: All send stock prices up and down.

During bubbles, extensive media coverage will lead you to be overconfident in your ability to pick stocks. If you are caught up in the herd hysteria, you may even reach a sense of grandiosity, believing yourself an investment genius. Addiction can take over as you constantly seek the high of easy money.

A sudden drop in stock prices triggers more troubling emotions. Some investors panic and sell everything. Panic is highly discouraged by those who make a living selling stocks. Investors who panic and sell out often feel guilty that they went against the advice of investment professionals. However, panic is the clearest sign that stocks are outside your comfort zone. A good panic can save you decades of trouble. Investors who panicked and sold in 1929 got over the guilt and had no regrets for the next 21 years. Investors who panicked in 1966, 1970, and 1974 got over the guilt and had no regrets until the mid-1980s.

Failure to panic in a crash is more troublesome. Tech stock investors who did not get out in April 2000 know these feelings well. Holding on through a crash will lead to depression and a sense of inferiority.

Longer bear markets lead to confusion, free-floating fear, resentments, and regrets. Those who failed to panic in 1966, 1970, and 1974 suffered until the 1980s bull market became fully established in 1985. Investors who hold on during long bear markets feel helpless, unable to stay in the market and sit with the pain of loss, yet unable to get out for fear of missing a great rise in prices. These emotions may last many years.

Stockbroker relationships are breaking up

As if it is not difficult enough to deal with employees siphoning off profits and market forces you cannot control, stocks are bought through a commission-hungry broker. A broker can be an individual you talk to, a telephone system, or a Web site. Nevertheless, your relationship with a broker can be troubling.

A broker makes money each time you buy or sell a stock. The broker profits from both commissions and the spread between the buy and sell price. For example, if you sell 1,000 shares of DUD for $10 each, you pay a commission ranging from $5 at a deep discount online broker to $200 at a full-service broker. The buyer of your shares pays anywhere from $10.02 a share to $10.20 a share. The difference between your selling price and the purchaser's buying price is the spread. The broker and others pocket the spread in addition to your commissions and the purchaser's commissions. It is in your broker's interest for you to make as many transactions as possible. It is not in your interest, because every transaction costs you money.

Many investors go to full-commission brokers for stock research, investment advice, and financial planning. Today, online discount brokers also provide these services. Unfortunately, most brokerage information is designed to sell more product more often, not to improve your financial position.

Wall Street has always known that buyers are primarily interested in stocks that increase in value. Profiting from declines is un-American. The easiest sell is a stock or fund that has already gone up. You will naturally be more confident that a stock or fund that has gone up will continue to do so. A broker will show you a select list of stocks that have strong momentum. Your overconfidence will hurt you. Studies show that stocks that have good streaks soon revert to the mean. While your broker is sure to know this, he will not disclose it to an optimistic buyer. He also has other sales tools.

Brokers know that you want researched stocks recommended by experts. That is why you came to them to begin with. Each brokerage house, therefore, has its own experts rating stocks just for you. When brokers rate stocks, on average more than 65 percent are rated buy, less than 35 percent are hold, and less than 1 percent are rated sell. Every broker, therefore, has a long list of buys to show you, several of which are certain to piqué your interest.

Unfortunately, buy ratings have a dual purpose. Buy ratings sell stock to you and they sell services to companies issuing stock and bonds. In 2000, brokers made more than $30 billion dollars helping companies issue stocks and bonds. These stocks and bonds are always given buy ratings. That keeps the client coming back; it may or may not keep you coming back.

Studies show that buy-rated stocks have random returns on average no better than the market. Frequently they serve to prop up stock prices temporarily so insiders can cash out their stock options at a profit before the collapse. Insiders have to act quickly, though. According to a 2001 study by Investors.com, buy ratings on IPOs by the analysts of the underwriting firm lead to losses six months later of greater than 50 percent.

Investors also go to their broker for comfort and support during the markets down periods. Unfortunately, a full-service broker is not a financial counselor or a psychologist, but a salesperson looking for a commission. He will always have a product to sell you in an attempt to ease your discomfort.

Margin calls, stop-loss orders, and sweep accounts: how to destroy a good night's sleep

Margin is particularly troublesome for optimistic investors. For every dollar of stock you own, your broker will "let" you borrow up to 50 cents to buy more shares. While 100 shares of a company sounds good to you, 150 shares, putting down the same amount of your savings, sounds like a bargain. Of course, there is interest to pay on the loan, but the optimist reasons that the inevitable rise in the stock price will more than compensate for the interest and will accommodate an easy repayment of the loan when necessary.

In practice, though, things often go quite differently. Should the company temporarily swoon, you will get a call from your broker advising you that the loan is now due and you need to either come up with more cash or he will sell out your shares, at a loss, and cover the margin. Now a particularly optimistic type will find more cash, buy more shares, and set himself up for an even bigger fall. Many optimists have lost their life savings from a series of these episodes. Lawsuits inevitably follow.

In particularly bad markets, you are more likely get a call stating that the matter has already been taken care of and you now own only 50 shares of this company, but you no longer owe the broker a dime. This may be fortunate as it avoids the opportunity for you to put up more of your cash. However, should the company immediately recover and soar, lawyers will argue for you in court that you were not given proper notice and an opportunity to cover the deficit, which you certainly would have done.

In every margin scenario, you may note, the broker collects larger commissions and more spreads than in a simple purchase-and-hold scenario. More shares are used in the transaction, plus the transaction inevitably involves a purchase, a sale, and margin interest.

Overconfidence in your investment ability is the main cause of margin investing. It is not a coincidence that the highest margin on record, $279 billion dollars, occurred at the peak of the NASDAQ in March 2000. Five years of 20 percent plus returns led investors to believe they could handle margin. Margin investing is best left to speculators or those with an admitted desire to lose their fortune. Optimists will be happier with a buy-and-hold strategy. Even after the worst bear market, they will still own their stocks, assuming no bankruptcies, and have the opportunity to again hope for a great rise.

Cautious investors often place stop-loss orders on their account. These orders sell out your shares should they decline by the amount of pain you anticipate you are willing to endure. Stop-loss orders are supposed to make an unmanageable situation manageable. Brokers encourage this as stock fluctuations inevitably trigger sales creating more commissions and spreads. In a market break, the sell point may be much lower than the level you specify. For example, on a surprising corporate announcement, it is common for prices to gap down by $10 or more. Your stop loss may have only been down $2, but you will be sold out at the next trade, $10 lower. Of course, you always have the opportunity to buy back in again for more commissions and increasingly wide spreads. Stop-loss orders often lead to anger and frustration as an attempt to bring order to an unmanageable situation fails for you, yet enriches your broker.

Brokerage accounts also offer you a "parking place" for your cash. These are sweep accounts: money market funds that collect dividends and the change leftover from trades. In the old days, dividend checks and change were sent to your home and you had the onerous task of depositing them in your checking account. The sweep accounts are marketed as a great convenience to you. In fact, they are a great convenience to your broker as they gather your funds within short distance of the trading desk. Again, particularly optimistic types should have the dividends sent home. Maybe there is only $1,000 at stake, but would you rather have a new couch to lie on during the bear market or would you prefer to whittle it away in commissions, spreads, and poor stock picks?

Web relationships get tangled

Many investors try to avoid these troublesome relationships by using online brokers. Online investing is promoted as fun. Chat rooms, IPOs, after-hours trading, 24-hour research: The message is: meet interesting people and make quick, easy money. The results are not any better than using a live-body broker.

Studies show switching to low-commission, online brokers leads to over-confidence. Stocks are bought and sold online in seconds. Online research takes hours if done quickly, days and weeks if done properly. Online investors skip the research and go directly to the trading page. This causes excessive trading, which quickly adds up to excess commissions, large spreads, great unhappiness, and poor results. A few investors become addicted to trading.

Investors using online brokers often turn to chat rooms to get comfort during volatile markets. Chat rooms are full of investors trying to promote their own shares. Their agenda is to get you out of your shares and into theirs at ever-higher prices. Rumors and mass hysteria are treated as fact in chat rooms. Your gullibility will hurt you.

Web portals promote thoughtless online trading. Web portals are paid by online brokers for each customer they send to the broker. Portals run "news" stories about stocks and then include links in the story to online brokers where you can quickly buy or sell the stock. If you give credence to printed material formatted as news, you are likely to be drawn into making online trades by a Web portal.

Online brokers trigger impulse buying. Impulse buyers do not even check the latest corporate news. The availability of cash or margin triggers purchases of any stock or fund that looks fun, sure, prestigious, or attractive. In seconds, the buy is executed and the impulse over. Remorse often follows.

Only investors with good research skills, independent attitudes, and patience are happy with online brokers. Others are outside their comfort zone. Impulse buyers should stay away from stocks in all forms. Real estate, oil and gas, and other asset classes are better routes to happiness.

Money managers dance better for a price

Money managers will handle your stock investments for a fee. This fee is in addition to the commissions and spreads you must pay a broker. Money managers cannot execute stock transactions. Some money management fees are a percentage of the value of your account. A money manager takes his fee whether your account increases or decreases in value. A money manager's primary interest is in retaining your account as long as possible so the steady fees continue to flow.

Money managers are experts at analyzing stocks. However, they often make the same emotional mistakes that you would make. Money managers got caught up in the tech mania of 1999-2001, as did individual investors. Overconfidence led them to trade too often and regret avoidance causes them to hold losers too long. Overconfidence also led others to invest in foreign and emerging market stocks that are outside their area of expertise. In 1987, money managers and other professional investors institutionalized overconfidence. They invented and bought portfolio insurance; this led directly to the crash of 1987.

However, money managers keep accurate, detailed records of your returns. They are unlikely to churn your account as commissions and spreads do not benefit them and may drive you away.

On the other hand, money managers may recommend you keep your account with a full-service broker and pay high commissions on the pretext that you will get better executions and they will use the research. In fact, brokers recommend clients to them in exchange for the promise that the client will continue to use the brokers' overpriced services. High commission discount brokers even set up pools of money managers that agree to keep clients with them in exchange for referrals.

Most money managers are astute salespeople. They have slick brochures and charts showing why they are better than the competition. They are not above using guilt and intimidation to keep you with them. They will also influence you to keep your money in their area of expertise. In the current decade, real estate prospects are better than stock prospects. You will find no stock money managers suggesting that their clients move assets into real estate.

Many people like money managers because it personalizes the stock market. Brokers are too busy to chat. Many money managers will go to lunch with you, swap stories about the children and college, and tell amusing anecdotes about the market. All too often, though, as money managers grow, they ignore their individual clients and focus on their large institutional clients. After a few years, your only relationship may be through the dry reports they send you.

For those of you who want to stay in denial about your stock investments, a money manager, for a fee, is a better choice than a broker free to churn your account. Churning will cost you and reduce your returns more than a money manager's quarterly fee.

A money manager is not a psychologist for the difficult years. A money manager's primary interest is in keeping your account, not helping you with your emotions. When the market and your account crash, a money manager is unlikely to admit his responsibility in loading up on overpriced stocks at the wrong time. More likely, he will attribute the loss to forces over which he is powerless and recommend you hold on for the certain recovery. Though recovery is never certain, and often takes decades, the money manager will be paid during the wait. Or the money manager might recommend a shift into less volatile bonds to quell your nerves. Typically, bonds require little research and monitoring for the money manager, and often they are chosen just as bond prices have peaked.

Your biggest liability working with a money manager is your sense of loyalty. You must be willing to cut and run when it becomes apparent that your money manager is not performing. Your ego also gets the best of you here. Beginning a conversation with "My money manager says..." indicates a degree of wealth and sophistication. "My index fund..." will only elicit boredom. Denial is not your friend either. You must analyze what your money manager is doing, get second opinions, and question him directly. People pleasers will have difficulty here.

The feelings are not mutual

Overwhelmed by the prospect of buying individual stocks, you may turn to mutual funds. Mutual funds are marketed as a simple way to own a diversified portfolio managed by a professional. Unfortunately, mutual funds are confusing and complex.

Confusion is rampant. There are as many mutual funds as there are individual stocks. Just when you think you have a fund picked out, the fund manager changes, the investment style is altered, and a load is imposed to purchase the former no-load fund. There are hundreds of styles and types of funds: micro cap, small cap, medium cap, and large cap, value, growth, blend, income, leveraged, unleveraged, closed-end, open-end, and so on.

Taxes are a mess. Those who buy the fund the day before the tax date have to pay taxes on capital gains that occurred before they owned the fund. Those who sell that day avoid the taxes even though they owned the fund while the gains occurred. Those who buy a day after the tax date have no taxes but a different cost basis even though they paid the same price for shares as those who bought before. Multiple systems can be used to declare your taxes and adjust your basis when you sell shares.

Calculating returns and comparing returns to other funds is equally complex. Unless you bought on January 1 and reinvested all dividends and capital gains, your returns and those in fund reports, the paper, and the magazines will be different. Ask yourself: How much complexity and confusion am I comfortable with? On these two criteria alone, mutual funds are outside the comfort zone of many investors.

What were you thinking when you bought that fund?

Seeking help, you may approach a broker to recommend funds. Unfortunately, regret is likely to follow. A broker's main interest is in loads and other commissions from frequent mutual fund sales. Loads of 5.75 percent are common. On a $10,000 investment, you are paying $575. You can buy an entire financial plan from a fee-only financial planner for less. If over the years you buy $100,000 of mutual funds, you will pay loads of $5,750. The sum of $5,750 buys several lifetimes of financial plans complete with tax savings ideas, estate planning tips, and zero-load mutual fund picks. However, unless you ask specifically and insist on an answer, you will not know the dollar amount you are paying for the privilege of buying a mediocre fund.

Loads can be paid on purchase of a fund (a front-end load) or on the sale of the fund (a back-end load) or both. A broker will use confusion and complexity against you.

Back-end loads may appear to be a good deal to you. Each year you hold the fund, the load goes down. After a year or two, the broker will recommend you switch funds. Many reasons can be given. You can avoid a taxable gain that will be distributed to you if you hold on. A management change or a style change has taken place. There is always a reason to switch funds. So you agree and pay a smaller back-end load and get a new back-end load fund. Two things are happening that you do not realize: First, each year you hold the fund you are paying larger expenses to management than someone who purchased front-end load shares; the back-end load only goes down as you pay it down. Second, your broker gets a larger, but secret, upfront load from the mutual fund company for selling back-end load funds than for selling front-end load funds.

Brokers will offer you many share classes with many varieties of loads. Funds can have A, B, C, D, and E classes. You will never fully understand why one is better than the other, nor why your broker wants you to switch from one fund to another or from one class to another. The reality is that with each purchase and switch, she gets another nice commission. People pleasing will hurt you here.

Even if you are able to find satisfactory funds on your own or with a broker, you may still have an uncomfortable experience.

Then there is the question of volatility

Mutual funds are diversified. Diversification is supposed to create steady returns. I simply do not believe it does.

Mass psychology reigns in mutual fund investing. By definition, a mutual fund is a herd of mindless investors led by an adored mutual fund manager. Mutual fund complexes promote their newest and hottest fund. Investors pour cash into the fund. The manager's ego soars. He buys more of the same stocks that drew in investors, puffing up the price of the stocks and the return from the fund. The hot fund is discovered by the financial press and more money pours in, more stock is purchased, and returns look even better. When all the buyers are in, a chat room rumor declares the fund and its stocks as over-valued, investors panic about redeeming shares, the fund manager is forced to sell at any price to meet redemptions further depressing stock values and the fund asset price, which panics more investors who redeem and send shares lower still. The depressed fund manager then abandons his old investment style, unloads the rest of the stocks at still lower prices, and moves into stuff remaining shareholders have no interest in owning. They redeem and send prices down again.

Investors experienced a classic example of this roller coaster during the 1999–2001 period. Growth and tech funds got hot and then abandoned. Value funds and energy funds were abandoned and then got hot. Fund managers were not hurt, though. Fund managers' pay increased by 35 percent during the period. In the mid-1990s, financial sector funds got hot and then were abandoned in the late 1990s. In 1997, real estate funds were hot, setting up investors for two years of losses in 1998 and 1999.

Some funds have learned to avoid wild swings in value. They do so not for your benefit, but for theirs. The goal of fund management firms is to gather and hold ever-larger amounts of your money. Fund managers are paid a percentage of funds under management. Fees are not based on returns or other criteria that benefit you. The larger the fund, the larger the fee. Primarily, though, fund managers must assure that funds never close. And in fact, they rarely do. Since 1970, the number of funds has declined in only one year, 1975. Even in bear markets, the number of funds grows. This game is too good to give up, for the fund managers. The average fund manager earns more than $430,000 per year, despite the fact that Morningstar data shows that the average fund manager has never outperformed the market over a single five-year period.

Mediocre funds with low volatility tend to grow their assets under management for decades. You may be happy to pay fees for mediocre results as long as you avoid the roller coaster. Or, you may feel the fund takes advantage of your loyalty. You may find that mutual funds cause resentment. This is not surprising. Your loyalty *is* being manipulated.

And I thought my family was bad

Fund organizations run many funds. They call themselves fund "families." Studies show that marketing, not high returns, increases funds under management over the long-term. The fund families send you newsletters and have Web sites. Every article is designed to encourage you to ignore the results you have gotten and buy more product. Your mailbox will also be stuffed with bulletins about new funds, account statements, proxy statements, and tax statements. The more money you have with the family, the higher the level of service and status you can achieve within the family. You can move up from ordinary to preferred to gold to platinum to admiralty.

Switching funds within the fund group is convenient and quick. To switch from a rival fund, they will even do all the paperwork for you. But moving out of the family is discouraged. If you are dissatisfied with one of their funds, they hope your sense of loyalty and desire for convenience will cause you to buy another fund within the family. Retaining your mutual funds is their primary goal.

Some funds close to new investors. This gives existing investors the illusion that they own an exclusive product, which discourages them from selling. Some funds also impose penalties for early withdrawals. This keeps your money under management and creates a steady income stream for the fund manager.

As with any good dysfunctional family, there are many secrets. You cannot find out what stocks your fund owns more than every six months, and then only 45 days after the six-month period ends. Nor can you get any information explaining why one manager was fired and another hired. Even mutual fund watchdogs such as Lipper and Morningstar cannot obtain this information. It is as if this is not your money but the family's money.

If you have family abandonment issues, mutual fund investing will be troublesome. Seeking approval and support for your emotional deficiencies will cause you to stay with poor funds when better returns are available elsewhere. Severe depression could follow.

Is it socially responsible to keep your fund manager in new cars?

Socially responsible mutual funds are an extreme example of asset gatherers using your values and neediness to turn you into a profit center for them. Socially responsible funds buy companies that they deem good corporate citizens or that follow certain religious or moral guidelines. They tend to avoid tobacco stocks, companies that discriminate or do not hire union workers, firearms and weapons manufacturers, and companies that pollute the environment.

While you are under the illusion your money is doing good, mutual fund companies operate on the hard fact that socially responsible fund investors do not trade funds and have low standards for investment return. These funds all buy the same stocks and produce the same mediocre returns, but their asset bases grow steadily. In recent years, socially responsible funds have been among the fastest growing asset gatherers. More importantly, your investment does not go directly to the company doing "good." Your cash is used to buy shares from other stockholders who are tired of the company. A direct investment in a socially responsible enterprise or in a public offering of new shares is rare. When you discover that your money is enriching fund managers, not you or your causes, you may feel betrayed. If stocks are outside your comfort zone, you will feel better giving directly to the endeavor you support and investing the rest of your funds within your comfort zone.

Is the index the right finger to be pointing?

For investors tired of watching mutual fund managers make lousy decisions and underperform the market, mutual fund families invented the index fund. The manager of the index fund buys and holds the stocks in the market index. Index funds return exactly what the market returns. Index funds have become extremely popular in the last decade.

As index funds increase in popularity, many non-index funds also imitate the indexes. Increasingly, more and more funds buy the same stocks, have exorbitant marketing expenses, and have the same goal: increasing funds under management. Stock selection is motivated by this goal. A fund full of unknown stocks will not be recommended by financial planners or understood by the public. Unusual funds are quickly labeled "too risky" and disappear.

Mutual fund families comb through the stock picks of each fund and assure that a minimum number of the popular index stocks are present. Managers who vary too far are reprimanded and eventually fired if they do not conform.

Fund managers also conform in other ways. Most managers pick stocks by the numbers: P/E ratios, earning growth rate, EBITDA to enterprise value, and so on. Hundreds of studies have shown that you cannot outperform the market looking solely at numbers. Insight is required. But insight can cost a manager his job and a $500,000 annual salary. Picking stocks by the numbers as does everyone else, keeps those paychecks rolling in.

In interviews and slick marketing brochures, mutual fund managers boast that they have one-on-one contact with company managers. Unfortunately for you, every mutual fund manager talks to the same company managers at your expense. Trips to New York, Boston, Silicon Valley, and Los Angeles are paid for by you. Investment conferences in Las Vegas, Honolulu, and Hong Kong cost you even more money. Because all the fund families talk to all the companies and go to all the conferences, no one gains any insight and all return home to the same numbers.

Fund gathering, job security, and indexing has resulted in most funds, index and non-index, owning the same stocks. Overowned stocks have huge market capitalization. It requires larger and larger purchases of stock to move prices up. In essence, $100 million in new money will increase the value of a $1 billion stock by 10 percent; a $100 billion stock will only increase in value by 0.1 percent.

Index fund investors and pseudo-index fund investors must be prepared for a decade of mediocre returns. Stock investors looking for the fast lane will find it clogged. Frustration and other symptoms of unmanageability will be common. Should indexing lose popularity, returns will turn negative as investors seek alternatives. If the herd abandons the index funds for money market funds, bonds, real estate, or other asset classes, all the emotions of a panic can be expected. If you are an independent thinker, you are best off avoiding mutual funds.

Long-term mutual fund holders often drift into indifference. After a few years, they have no sense of connection with their money. All fund statements and mailings are glanced at and filed or thrown out. In the back of their minds, they know there is something they ought to be doing but having put it off for many years, they simply leave it be. Mutual funds in IRAs and 401(k)s are often abandoned for decades. On retirement, the holders are shocked at how little money has accumulated.

Active investors become resentful of fund managers. Fund managers' salaries are insulated from fund results. Salaries rise in bad years as well as good. With no stake in the outcome of their investment decisions, fund managers' interest and yours are opposed. Fund managers make more money than doctors, lawyers, and all but the CEOs of the largest corporations. Yet their results are no better than random picks from the stock tables.

Alternatives to mutual funds

For discouraged investors, other products are available. Closed-end funds (CEFs) are mutual funds that are sold on the exchanges like stocks. Open-end mutual funds are sold directly to investors; every dollar invested adds to the assets under management and management fees. After an initial public offering to raise capital, CEFs are bought and sold between investors at whatever price investors are willing to pay. The price of a CEF can be higher or lower than the value of the stock held by the fund. CEF managers are only able to offer new shares if returns have been good and the fund becomes popular. However, the prices of CEFs are volatile.

Closed-end funds are subject to mass psychosis. When certain stocks are hot, CEFs owning those stocks can sell for several times net asset value (NAV). Investors often experience overconfidence and grandiosity. When these stocks are unpopular, CEFs plunge to a fraction of NAV.

When CEFs linger below NAV for long periods of time, frustration sets in. Often shareholder suits are filed to open up the fund and distribute assets at NAV. CEFs are also subject to management changes and style changes. In addition, CEFs are often taken over by outside management companies and converted into larger funds. Spreads and commissions on CEFs are often painful. Closed-end funds are outside the comfort zone of most mutual fund investors.

Exchange traded funds (ETFs) are CEFs that own a set group of stocks, often those in an index such as the S&P 500 or the Dow Jones utilities. Most ETFs are also convertible into the underlying shares such that they always trade at or near NAV. The main issue with ETFs is that they only own the overpriced, overowned stocks in the index. When the last buyer is in for overpriced stocks, returns are mediocre at best and volatility increases. However, ETFs, unlike index funds, are traded all day long. Overconfident investors will trade them, running up commissions and spreads.

Internet companies now offer, for a fee, selected groups of individual stocks. These preset stock portfolios are tailored to attract a wide range of investor whims and are designed to give the investor the illusion of control. With a mutual fund you are taxed on gains you did not incur and can lose value because other investors panic and sell. Internet portfolios allow you to control your gains and do not subject you to the whims of fund managers and fund management companies. Unfortunately, as a group, most of these portfolios will have the same swings as the market. These portfolios are full of the same overowned, overbought stocks that fill mutual funds. When the last buyer is in, return will be mediocre and volatility high. A mutual fund panic will cause your portfolio to drop just as it would if you owned a mutual fund. Powerlessness can lead to anxiety, numbness, depression, and free-floating fears as with any stock product.

Fee advice

For a fee, newsletter writers rate individual stocks and funds. Most newsletter writers are optimistic sorts who like to predict ever-rising stock prices. A few are perennial bears. Newsletters sell from $60 a year to more than $1,000. The higher priced newsletters claim to have better information. Newsletter writers on a hot streak sell more copy; some become household names for a few years until their streak runs out. Extensive studies of newsletters show less than 20 percent outperform the market. Higher priced newsletters are no more accurate than cheap newsletters. Most newsletters die within a few years of sending out their first batch of predictions.

Investors looking for certainty in an unpredictable market turn to newsletters. Their authors become gurus. Many a fortune has been lost along the way. The gold bug gurus of 1975-1980 continued to recommend half or more of a portfolio in gold throughout the 1980s as gold lost more than 65 percent of its value.

Investors who choose among newsletter recommendations and supplement newsletter research with their own research will benefit. One or two good picks can be worth the price of a subscription.

On the other hand, as a newsletter subscriber, you may believe you are in an exclusive club with special knowledge about the market. This sense of grandiosity can be hazardous to your financial and mental health. If you find yourself continuing to follow the advice of a guru despite horrendous losses, turn directly to Steps 2 and 3 of this book.

What value is value? Are we talking personal growth or portfolio growth?

One of the great marketing tools for stocks is the promise that there is a product that will work for every investor. Companies, brokerage firms, and mutual fund houses are constantly putting out new products to sell to discouraged investors. Financial professionals never miss an opportunity to sell a gullible investor a stock. They have invented a wrench to fit every nut.

No stock style or category eliminates the basic problem with stocks. Style is supposed to take the sting out of investing. Unfortunately, all stocks, regardless of category, are subject to the whims of the herd.

Utility stocks are marketed as steady income vehicles akin to Treasury bonds, yet they are often as volatile as tech stocks. Utility stock prices were cut in half when Three Mile Island threatened to ruin the power business. They were whacked again when deregulation eliminated their monopoly position in many markets. Recently, increased gas prices sent the once steady and reliable PG&E into bankruptcy and put Southern California Edison on the brink of bankruptcy.

Each type of stock creates its own emotional complexities.

Preferred stock was one of the marketer's first products. When common stock investors realized that in financial stress, the company canceled dividends but paid bond interest, they sold stock and bought bonds. Companies then began to issue preferred stock with fixed dividends. Preferred stock dividends are paid when a company is in stress, but in bankruptcy, preferred stock is canceled, the same as common stock. Few investors are comfortable with this netherworld between bonds and stocks. The complexity of determining how to value preferred stock keeps many investors away. These days stock is considered a pure capital gains vehicle and bonds are used for income.

Stocks that collapse in price were once known as dogs and cats. Brokers started calling them value stocks and were able to peddle them to individuals and mutual fund managers. Unfortunately, value stocks are highly unstable. Many are troubled companies headed for bankruptcy. Others are turning around. In today's markets, value stocks can quickly become overpriced. Then value fund managers sell them to growth managers. Investors looking to value stocks for low volatility will not find it.

Growth stocks are overpriced stocks that are hyped as having huge earnings potential. Growth investors are gullible sorts who believe a few years of fabulous growth will be repeated for decades. They are willing to pay any price for this dream.

The tech mania of 1999 was an extreme example of this magical thinking. Growth investors convinced themselves that untested Internet companies would take over the American economy in a few years. Tech mania has a long and sad history in stock investing. Tech mania generally ends badly. Railroad stocks got up a full head of steam and then jumped the track in the late 1800s. Electricity plays and auto stocks had huge booms and busts in the early 1900s. Long-term studies show that tech stocks do no better than the overall market. However, they are subject to periods of extreme volatility. Tech stocks, when the mania is on, double and triple in a few months. Then they lose 95 percent of their value in the crash. Tech stocks are for dreamers and speculators, not investors. People who do not mind losing a few thousand dollars for the potential of extreme wealth are comfortable with tech stocks. Investors with low self-esteem, who may throw good money after bad, should stay away from tech stocks and other growth stocks.

Growth investing has an addictive quality. Just as the alcoholic rationalizes away hangovers and arguments in the belief that the next bottle will bring happiness, the growth investor rationalizes away P/Es, asset prices, burn rates, and all other measures of financial value for the dream of finding the next Microsoft. When growth slows and the stock price collapses, unhealthy investors try to get even. Rationalizing away the recent collapse, they invest their remaining funds as well as new savings and borrowings. A fresh collapse can then send them into deep depression.

Only investors aware that they are buying a fantasy will be comfortable with growth stocks. Idea people have fun with growth stocks. There is always a new idea that could grow into a world-beating company. Number people suffer from growth stocks. Number people do fancy calculations of sales, earnings, book value, return on capital, and growth rates to determine the likely price of a stock in five or 10 years. Number people are heartbroken when all their fancy calculations turn into losses.

Worker bees will have fun with micro cap stocks. These are companies too small to be included in the indexes or to be owned by the mutual funds. No analysts cover these companies. If you enjoy discovering stocks no one has ever heard of and are interested in working hard at finding and analyzing these companies, the financial rewards are high. You will not be able to toss out the names of your stocks at parties because no one will know what you are talking about. Patience is required because these things take time to be found by other investors and bid up in price. This is often a lonely but rewarding business.

Investors without patience or research skills may be tempted to buy micro cap mutual funds. Unfortunately, the micro cap mutual funds have all the problems of other mutual funds: they all buy the same stocks, get caught up in manias such as tech mania, tax you for gains that were not yours, siphon off fees, and focus on gathering assets and marketing rather than increasing your returns. And micro cap funds buy such large amounts of stock that they bid up the price of shares as they buy, then they depress the price as they sell. Micro cap mutual funds have many built-in resentments.

Initial public offerings (IPOs)

Before coming to market, initial public offerings (IPOs) must issue a prospectus describing the company and its risks. Virtually every prospectus I've ever seen is written in unreadable legalese. I doubt any analysts not associated with the investment banks that wrote them bother to even glance at them. The investment banks are paid unbelievable sums to underwrite IPOs. Underwriters can make as much as $20 billion a year issuing IPOs. After reading the prospectus, the analyst produces reports promoting the issue. The report gets picked up in the chat rooms and the hype is on.

IPO prices can be manipulated in many ways by the issuers and the underwriters. In addition to analyst reports, popular IPOs are sold by allocation only to those willing to either buy additional shares after the IPO or give additional business to the underwriters. With buyers in place before the initial offering, the offering price can be raised increasing returns to the issuer and the underwriter. When the price pops on the opening, insiders are given the opportunity to unload shares at tremendous profits.

The only non-insiders who are happy with IPOs are volatility junkies. In a bull market, many IPOs double and triple in price the day of the offering. When their popularity wanes, they drop back to the initial price or lower. In a bear market, new IPOs are rare. The few that come to market often collapse below the IPO price. However, the investment bankers retain their billions of profits.

IPOs can be thrilling and depressing. The winners make great chat on the Internet and conversation at parties. Every once in a while, a winner will grow into a great company such as Microsoft. The losers are just part of the gamble for real speculators. Most investors will find IPOs outside their comfort zone.

Technical analysis paralysis

Seeking to take emotion out of investing, stock analysts have invented many systems of technical analysis. Technical analysts look only at numbers. Most believe a thorough study of stock price and volume patterns alone should allow the prediction of future prices. Some technical analysts study more factors than price and volume. All build elaborate charts and read them for clues to the future. Often, extensive computer modeling and game playing systems are employed. Economic factors, stockbroker pressure, the brother-in-law's inside information, the CEO's cold, and other factors are ignored.

Technical analysis is great for number people. You can play with endless formulas to analyze past trends hoping to predict the future. However, technical analysis is best employed on other people's money. Then you can remain objective and emotionless.

All the studies of technical analysis show that it is ineffective. Used on your own money, you are likely to have strong feelings as losses mount.

Technical analysts get hot streaks. Famous analysts appear on all the business TV shows. They attract a large following of believers. Their pronouncements often move markets. Then, after a series of bad calls, they are considered buffoons. They still appear on the TV shows but are abused by interviewers for their bad calls.

Investors who seek certainty are attracted to these investment gurus. The gurus sell expensive newsletters and give expensive seminars. Investors who cannot handle the unmanageability and powerlessness in stock investing are willing to pay guru fees. Besides fees, technical analysis usually requires much buying and selling that incurs commissions and spreads. Usually, followers find the gurus at the height of their popularity. This is when they are receiving the most publicity and are near the end of their hot streak. New converts then plunge into the inevitable cold streak and lose large sums of money.

Emotion cannot be avoided in investing. We are all attached to our money. When values soar, our egos soar. Huge losses plummet all of us into anxiety, depression, regrets, resentments, and free-floating fear. No investment system will ever take all the emotion out of investing. The trick is to find investments within your emotional comfort zone. If you find technical analysis fun, despite recurring losses, then it is in your comfort zone. If you find the losses depress you too much, technical analysis is not within your comfort zone.

Shorting stock

Investors looking for a real thrill ride may be interested in shorting stock. Normally you purchase a stock at its current price and then sell it at some future date at an unknown price. You are hoping the future price is higher. Stock exchanges allow you to reverse the process; you can sell a stock that you do not own at the current price as long as you promise to purchase the stock at some future date at an unknown price. By selling now, you have locked in your sales price. You hope that the future purchase price will be lower so you can make profit. For example, if you sell ABC short today for $50, you hope to buy it in six months for $25 realizing a gain of $25. If six months from now ABC sells for $75 and you cover your short at that price, you lose $25.

There are two crucial differences between going short and going long: going short requires going against the will of the vast majority of investors and the potential losses from going short are unlimited.

Most investors are optimists. They believe over the long-term stock prices go up. The financial services industry and the financial press cater to this optimism. There are tremendous commissions, spreads, and management fees to be made from optimistic investors. Best-selling investment books usually spout tales of compounding stock prices turning thousands of dollars into millions. Cautious investors are likely to take their money out of the market, cancel newsletters, and avoid investment books.

With optimism as the prevailing attitude, it is heretical to insist stock prices will decline, and sacrilegious to make money from declining stock prices. Shorts are vilified by the financial services industry and in the financial press. Mutual fund managers often declare their abhorrence of shorting stocks, lest any potential investor think them a traitor. Television interviewers hark on the shorts' mistakes, and often give them unfair coverage, if any. Intimidated by social pressure, few investors dare go short.

You must be an independent thinker capable of acting in spite of social ostracism if you wish to short stocks. Some will brand you a rebel. Few investors will be comfortable going short. Switching to real estate or oil and gas partnerships may be easier. Rather than being vilified by the equity culture, you will be ignored.

Even investors with the self-esteem to go short may not have the required emotional fortitude. The loss potential of going short is unlimited. Say you buy 1,000 shares of a stock at $10. Your potential loss, should it go bankrupt, is $10,000. On the other hand, sell 1,000 shares short at $10, the potential loss is unlimited. If the stock moves up to $20 and you cover, you lose $10,000. At $30, you lose $20,000. At $110, you lose $100,000 on a $10,000 investment. The seeming unlimited potential gain of stocks works against you. Anyone with difficulty admitting mistakes, taking losses, and moving on will be miserable shorting stock. If you are the type that holds on to losing positions waiting in pain to get out if you ever break even, you will be even more unhappy with shorts. Though stockbrokers are often blamed and sued in shorting cases, invariably the investor's lack of self-knowledge was the real culprit.

Employer stock

Employer stock is about loyalty, not investment return. Many 401(k) plans match contributions from employees with shares of employer stock. About a third of all 401(k) assets are company stock. Stock option plans allow employees to buy shares of employer stock at a discount. Stock ownership plans are funded entirely with employer stock. Tax benefits in these plans encourage the purchase of employer stock. Employees are also encouraged to buy employer stock outright. Advancement in the corporate structure requires playing by the rules.

Many employees also believe that they understand the company better than outsiders do. This often turns out to be pure overconfidence. Few employees know anything about stock analysis and evaluation. Their inside view often blinds them to competitive threats and negative market conditions. As a result, employees frequently have half or more of their investment assets in employer stock.

For employees who value loyalty more than investment return, this is fine. For other employees, this is a disaster. Individual stocks are highly volatile. You will need to adjust to wild swings in the value of your shares. If your retirement depends on the value of your company stock, you may be forced to retire later or not at all. Solid companies can quickly turn into a mess. Corporate troubles are usually accompanied by large layoffs. You may lose your job at the same time the stock collapses. Most employees will be happier selling company stock down to 5 percent or less of your portfolio. Sometimes in life, we have to choose between guilt and self-abuse. For most employees, guilt is the better choice.

Foreign and emerging market stocks

You can buy stock in developed countries such as Germany and the United States. Many emerging markets such as Venezuela and Thailand also have stock markets. You can buy their stocks individually on the U.S. markets or through a foreign brokerage account. You can also buy U.S.

mutual funds that specialize in foreign and emerging stocks. There are also CEFs and ETFs that own non-U.S. stocks.

Non-U.S. stocks have all the emotional content of U.S. stocks. Herd psychosis, powerlessness, issues with brokers and mutual funds, overconfidence, and all the rest are common in foreign investing. Foreign stocks also have additional traps we rarely encounter with local companies.

Foreign stocks are bought and sold in foreign currencies. Foreign companies make profits and losses in foreign currencies. Because you spend U.S. dollars, foreign stock prices must be translated into U.S. dollars before you can determine if you have any gains or losses. This adds volatility to foreign stock prices. If the Euro sinks by 15 percent and your German auto stock declines in Euros by 15 percent, you lose 30 percent in dollars. If the Euro rises by 15 percent and the auto stock rises by 15 percent, you gain 30 percent in dollars. A similar U.S. auto stock would only swing up and down 15 percent.

The volatility of foreign currency alone may place these stocks outside your comfort zone. In the Asian collapse of 1997-1998, most currencies declined by more than 50 percent and many stock markets collapsed by 50 percent in local currencies, leaving U.S. investors with 75 percent and greater dollar losses.

The range of loss is greater than in the United States. But the speed is also faster. The worst one-day loss in the overall U.S. market was 22 percent. Emerging markets have lost half their value in a single day. Some have closed and never reopened, essentially wiping out all values. If you find volatility disturbing, stocks, especially foreign and emerging market stocks, are outside your comfort zone.

In many non-U.S. markets, corporate employees and insiders have less respect for outside shareholders than they do here. If U.S. shareholders get too irritated, they can band together and oust management and other employees who are siphoning off all the earnings. In many overseas markets, insiders cannot be ousted, while minority shareholders may find their stock canceled or redeemed.

Few emerging markets have effective stock market regulation. In the United States and many developed countries, stocks cannot be bought and sold on the basis of secret corporate information. In emerging markets, this is common, even if it is technically illegal. It is also difficult in many emerging markets to cash out of profits when they do occur. In the United States, stock sales are settled in three days. In emerging markets, settlement dates and procedures can be vague and money is lost along the way. The level of unmanageability is much higher with emerging markets than in the United States.

Some investors who can process emotions quickly enjoy foreign stocks. Non-U.S. stocks are idea investments with great idea complexity. The romantic, foreign traveler who realizes the risk but enjoys the hunt can have fun here. Foreign and emerging markets are less picked over than the U.S. market. In the midst of the chaos, there are tremendous bargains. If you like to read about China and Israel, travel to Turkey and Paris, or think about Euros versus yen, then this may be in your comfort zone. For the foreign traveler, who is practically addicted to foreign investing, 50 stocks will provide a lifetime of entertainment. But most investors will be rattled by the volatility and dishonesty.

Even local investors are turned off by the irregularities overseas. Investors in most foreign and emerging markets invest in bank savings instruments, government bonds, and real estate. Only in the last five years has there been general interest in stocks. Huge American brokers, mutual funds, and investment banks see tremendous profits to be made from instilling an "equity culture" overseas. Not only can they sell products to overseas investors, but they can sell U.S. investors turned off by the U.S. market hot foreign and emerging market products.

Vast amounts of propaganda have been produced to instill equity culture overseas. The two pillars of the platform are that stocks are the best investment for the long-run and stocks are the only investment with returns high enough to save the shaky retirement systems of European and Asian countries. Respected newspapers and magazines looking for large ad revenues from the campaign have joined the chorus. Politicians looking for votes have enacted 401(k)-type legislation. Unfortunately, equity culture is not likely to make many investors happy.

There is no reason to believe that stocks will outperform real estate and other investments in the future. In the United States, stocks have existed for 200 years. Many non-U.S. markets are 50 years old or less. Real estate has been an investment class since the cave dwellers. The fact that U.S. stocks have a lead over bonds and are neck and neck with real estate over the last 200 years proves little about the future. Two hundred data points in 10,000 years of history is not conclusive when it comes to the United States. Less than 50 years is hardly any evidence about the future outside the United States. Equity culture will not save foreign pension systems. And it is not likely to make many American investors happy either. Resentments, fears, anxieties, and other built-in emotional traps make even prosperous investors miserable.

The equity culture gap

In the United States, financial institutions have succeeded in imposing stocks into the culture as the primary investment for the long-term. Legislatures have gone along to coddle voters. IRAs, 40l(k)s, and other tax-favored schemes can only be funded with stocks, bonds, and mutual funds; real estate, gold, and most other asset classes are not allowed. In the 1990s, the number of stock investors and the trading on stock exchanges tripled. There are many dark sides to this besides the fact that there is no conclusive proof that stocks will be the best investment in the future. Equity culture breeds stock jealousy, envy, and regret, which in turn create social tension and recessions. The recent tech boom and bust is one example.

During the tech bubble, many stock investors were jealous of the young entrepreneurs who, through IPOs, became instant millionaires. Many investors envied the employees who received stock options, rather than having to buy stock on the open market. Other investors regretted that they failed to buy the IPOs that doubled, tripled, and quadrupled. In a small asset class, with few investors, another's success becomes an inspiration rather than a regret. In stocks, these emotions churned up a fever to get in on the action. Businesses that serviced the new economy were so envious that they began to accept stock as payment for services rather than cash. Hardworking employees quit their jobs and became day traders. Companies paying good salaries added stock options to their compensation packages to retain envious employees. Insatiable investors agreed to pay exorbitant commissions and make unnecessary trades in exchange for a few IPO shares.

Unfortunately, with equity culture so widespread, the tech wreck destroyed far more than a few hundred ridiculously priced tech stocks. All those investors and companies sucked in by jealousy, envy, and regret were hurt. So too were nonparticipants. Regions of the country dropped into recession. Individuals with no savings lost their jobs. At least the Internet millionaires had homes and cars they could sell for cash until they found new professions.

All bull markets create the belief that stocks are a sure road to high profits. The 1990s bull market added the notion that though there will be ups and downs, in the long term, stocks always beat all other asset classes; in fact, everyone can have free money if they just buy stocks and hold on. The certainty with which this notion has been espoused has prevented investors from hearing a quiet inner voice. That little voice has been whispering for a long time: This cannot go on forever; a price must be paid for all these riches.

Stocks are the 800-pound gorilla of the investment world. Once you agree to dance with the gorilla, the dance is not over until the gorilla says it is. Freeing yourself from the equity culture is very difficult. Stock investors need to consider whether they have the ability to adapt to other investment classes if equities fail to produce positive returns.

Are stocks outside your comfort zone?

How does all this make you feel? Even if you have large profits in your stock account, has it been worth it?

Few investors have the emotional makeup to be happy in a long-term relationship with stocks.

A happy stock investor can process emotions quickly and act appropriately. He is not numb or emotionless in his investing. He sees losses in his portfolio, feels the pain, and the pain motivates him to do his research. He does not blindly hope to get out when he breaks even. He is realistic about conflicts of interest with employees and brokers. He takes action or determines not to act based on research, not stock prices. Numb investors avoid the pain of losses until they crack under stress. They are the ones who panic at the final bottom.

The happy mutual fund investor is aware of fund fees, turnover, taxes, trading costs, and sales pressure. After fully researching funds, she accepts reasonable costs as a tradeoff to allow her to focus on other areas of her life. She never buys a fund based on sales pressure or loyalty to the fund family. Rather, she owns funds on their merits. She feels her losses and her gains, and then makes buy and sell decisions based on fund fundamentals and not on fund prices.

The happy investor has many emotional ups and downs, but makes few trades. He recognizes that stock investing is a long-term commitment. He can sit for years on his stocks and funds and not make a single trade even though prices double and get cut in half. Meanwhile, he enjoys research and information gathering. The unhappy stock investor experiences these same ups and downs as trauma.

A happy stock investor has humility rather than overconfidence. She knows she does not know where market, stock, and fund prices are going. She lets herself be human, make mistakes. She learns from her mistakes. She understands that no one can invest perfectly. She is comfortable with uncertainty and estimates rather exactitudes. She knows when she has done enough research and is fine with the limits of her abilities. Once enough facts are in, she can take action, selling at losses rather than let them run for years, or closing out winners, once the trend appears broken.

He has a good dose of self-esteem and little need to please other people. He gathers information from many sources. He uses brokers, sales people, family, friends, work associates, and bosses as sources of information rather than conforming to their wishes that he buy or sell what they are promoting. He can view information objectively. He is an independent thinker. Even though it is discouraged, when his company matches his 401(k) contribution with company stock, he routinely sells the company stock to keep his allocation to 5 percent or less.

She is not in denial about what is happening in the market or her funds or stocks. She is not afraid of emotions. "My broker is handling it," "my mutual fund manager is an expert," "I have a money manager for that": All these forms of avoiding commitment and feelings are not for her. Denial leads to crisis. She is not interested in finding after the fact that the broker churned the account, the mutual fund manager was a rookie and got conned by the CEOs, or the money manager followed the herd into the tech bubble and tech wreck. She stays involved emotionally and intellectually.

Most importantly, the happy investor has the humility to change. The happy investor has the self-esteem to go counter-culture in the equity culture. When the big picture is clear, and stocks are in for another 10- to 15-year period of underperforming inflation, he can give up his identity as a stock investor and move on to another asset class. He can adjust to one of the many good alternatives to stocks.

Real estate

Few investors these days own commercial real estate, yet it fits the emotional profile of many people. Just to consider real estate you need to have high self-esteem. Many groups and individuals have vested interests in keeping you in stocks, including financial journalists. Commercial real estate articles are full of caveats and qualifications. You are warned that real estate requires time and attention and, according to them, stocks do not. They warn that overbuilding and deep recessions affect real estate and fail to warn that stock bubbles and mild recessions destroy stock returns.

Real estate is a good alternative to stocks. The happy real estate investor is a different animal than the happy stock investor. However, real estate is not for everybody.

A smoother ride

A sense of powerlessness, unmanageability, and helplessness are infrequent with real estate. Stock prices move quickly. An individual stock can lose half or more of its value in minutes. Real estate prices change slowly. There is very little change day to day or month to month. Typical real estate cycles are 10 years of moderate gains, followed by five years of flat returns, and then another 10 years of moderate gains.

Between 1988 and 1994, many investors lost money in real estate limited partnerships and real estate tax shelters (RELPs). These losses were very painful. Many investors vowed never to invest in real estate again. Unfortunately, they did not realize that their losses were not caused by real estate. Real estate returns during the period were slightly up. The huge expenses siphoned out of the RELPs by unscrupulous general partners caused the losses. General partners became multimillionaires. Limited partners lost most or all of their investment. General partners' greed was at fault, not the real estate markets.

The pain and resentment from losses can cause you to project negative feelings on an asset class rather than the actual cause of the loss. Most investors who lost money in RELPs blamed real estate rather than the general partners. If you lost money in RELPs and now believe that real estate is too risky for you but stocks are not, be sure to write about this in the exercises in Step 2.

Half the return from real estate comes from income and half from appreciation. Currently, all the return from stocks comes from appreciation. Income is more predictable than appreciation. Income simply requires that the tenants pay their rent. Appreciation requires that other investors bid up the price of the building. Studies by the National Council of Real Estate Fiduciaries show that since the 1970s, annual real estate prices range from down 10 percent to up 20 percent. Most years, prices are up 3 percent to 8 percent. In both down years and up years, prices are supplemented by income of 5 percent to 10 percent. Annual stock prices range from down 25 percent to up 35 percent. There is no income to dampen volatility in the down years. Slower movement and a smaller range of movement makes real estate more comfortable than stocks for many investors.

A real estate investor can control many factors that affect returns. Real estate is primarily influenced by local market dynamics. A corner building is usually better for retail than the interior buildings. The size of the parking lot, freeway access, high-tech wiring, and many other small factors affect rents and returns. By paying attention to detail, a real estate investor will find a sense of manageability. Despite paying attention to detail, stock investors can suddenly find their stock price cut in half.

Macro factors do affect real estate returns. The local economy is most important. Tenants disappear when the economy is bad. National factors can also affect returns. National interest rates determine local mortgage rates. When the federal government raises interest rates, financing new properties becomes more expensive.

Unlike stocks, with real estate, an active, flexible investor can mitigate just about every factor. Rents can be lowered below market to attract tenants. Adjustable rate mortgages can get you through a few years of high rates. However, inflexible or inactive investors will drop into a sense of powerlessness.

Many real estate investors fail to realize the market determines rents, utility costs, mortgage rates, and all other components of return. Inflexible investors will sit on half empty buildings for years waiting for "fair" rents rather than accept market rent. This invariably leads to a crisis point where the investor faces a foreclosure or punitive refinancing.

Simpler than stocks

A stockbroker will tell you to avoid real estate, because it is too complex and time-consuming. Stocks are marketed as simple, with no work required; just buy, and hold. In fact, the opposite is true.

Real estate is confusing and complex for the beginner. A first-time investor must have the humility to realize she does not know all the complexities. However, after a few years, real estate becomes very simple. Once she has figured out that Unit N rents for less than Unit M because it has less light, she will always know that. By contrast, stocks are ever-changing and ever-complex. A growth stock becomes a value stock, which turns into a momentum play until it files for bankruptcy.

The longer you invest in real estate, the simpler it becomes. The longer you invest in stocks, the more complex it becomes. Long-term stock investors ride up bubbles and down crashes, study ever-changing companies and economies, continuously pay management fees, try to simplify by focusing solely on price, and end up in a panic, selling at a loss. Long-term real estate investors raise rents, watch property appreciate, and find less work is required as returns increase.

Realtors do put sales pressure on you. Stories of fabulous appreciation and tiny down payments are common. People pleasing is an issue. You cannot buy to make your Realtor happy. However, this is less prevalent than with stocks where one phone call produces a trade. Real estate is not easily bought and sold. Financing must be arranged. You have to go over leases and tax records and accounts. Down payments are substantial commitments. Even extreme people pleasers are generally unwilling to go through all this just to be nice.

Real estate taxes are complex and confusing. Do-it-yourself investors do well with real estate except in this area. However, with the humility to ask for help, many accountants can work out the details for you. After a few years, you may be able to do your taxes yourself, assuming the tax laws haven't changed.

Mathematical skills are required for real estate. Accounting is not complex but it needs to be done regularly. High school math skills are more than adequate. Discipline is more important than advanced math skills. All income and expenses must be tracked. Future repairs and vacancies need to be planned for. Enjoying the accounting is ideal. However, a pure idea person with no math skills will do well with real estate as long as he hires an accountant.

Herd psychosis is an occasional problem with real estate. The United States had a bubble in large offices and apartment complexes in the 1980s. Individual investors were sucked in through tax shelters and limited partnerships.

Generally, real estate is cyclical, but not prone to bubbles. The 1980s bubble required the cooperation of the mortgage lenders and the Congress. Most of those buildings were built with little down, huge mortgages, and generous tax benefits for both investors and lenders. This lead to the collapse of many banks, S&Ls, and insurance companies. Currently, real estate lenders are not cooperating in pumping up a real estate bubble. Tax legislation is no longer favorable to real estate. While stocks are favored by the latest IRA and 401(k) changes, real estate remains restricted. It is not likely that we will see a real estate bubble in the next decade.

Fear of large sums

Many investors stay away from real estate because the sums of money involved scare them. A single-family rental can cost anywhere from $80,000 to $250,000. Apartments and office buildings range from $250,000 to several million dollars. Even with a 10-percent down payment, a $250,000 fourplex requires $25,000 out of pocket and a loan of $225,000.

Borrowing to buy real estate usually creates less fear than borrowing on margin to buy stocks. In real estate, most loans are secured by the property and the owner is not liable to pay the loan back if things go badly. The mortgage lender must take the property. In addition, a large down payment and the slow pace of real estate price changes generally eliminate any threat of foreclosure. An all-cash real estate purchase avoids the issue altogether.

Small down payments and no money down

With a small down payment, your down payment and your self-image are at stake. The threat to self-image is often the biggest obstacle to buying real estate with borrowed money. Many investors fear they will be viewed poorly by society if they are forced to give a building back to the bank. In practice though, many people revere those who take large risks with bank money rather than their own and then let the banks take the losses if all goes wrong. Other investors feel great guilt about returning buildings to the lender even though the loan was specifically negotiated with non-recourse terms.

Many investors have $25,000 to $250,000 invested in stocks. A bear market could wipe out the equivalent of many real estate down payments. On the other hand, bear markets do not cause foreclosure proceedings with the phone calls, letters, and legal documents coming at you. Margin stock investors are dealt with quickly. Often their stocks are gone before they get the notice. Foreclosures drag on for many months. Notices show up in newspapers. Fear of negative publicity is a common deterrent to real estate investing.

You may be lured by no-money-down real estate. These deals are not for everybody. You must be able to accept foreclosure proceedings as a regular part of your investment. Only distressed real estate is sold for no money down. Often, the purchaser becomes more distressed than the property. Good boundaries are required.

Many investors buy with no money down, discover the rents cannot cover the mortgage, maintenance, improvements, and other expenses, and pay out of pocket to keep the property alive. Then they discover that the neighborhood is deteriorating. Rents will not go up; they may go down. The property ends up in foreclosure. By this time, their no down payment property has cost thousands in carrying costs.

If you cannot handle foreclosures or will pay out of pocket to keep dead properties alive for decades, you are not going to be happy with no-money-down real estate.

The tenant is not your ailing mother

Real estate does require interpersonal skills. Happy stock investors can succeed solely by interacting with reading material and a computer. The real estate investor must interact with either tenants or a property manager, accountants, loan officers, Realtors, maintenance people, insurance sales-people, neighbors, and community authorities.

Tenant interactions are emotionally tricky. Tenants are interested in the lowest possible rent with the highest possible service. If you have guilt about being a landlord, it will be difficult. You will let tenants go weeks, months, even years without paying rent. You will fix problems that tenants are responsible to fix. You will let tenants rent without leases or insurance and leave yourself wide open for lawsuits. You will not raise rent to market levels but still improve the property. Or, you might just go into hiding and avoid the property, collect the rent by mail, and squeak by with whatever little profit you can get.

These problems are particularly acute in apartments and single-family homes. Guilty landlords think they are being noble by providing housing at below market rents. In fact, they are self-destructing. Their hard-earned savings are being wasted. Eventually their properties will be foreclosed on and the bank will get full-market rents.

You must be able to put your economic interest ahead of your tenants to be happy in real estate. An occasional rent concession is not a problem. A pattern of rent concessions is setting you up for the painful ego deflation of foreclosure.

Mortgage prison

Mortgage issues are not all caused by lack of self-esteem. Overconfi-dence and grandiosity are also problems.

In strong real estate markets, investors see real estate prices moving in only one direction: up. Overconfidence causes them to borrow as much as possible so they can buy a bigger building and make more money. They buy a $2,000,000 building with $100,000 down instead of a $200,000 building. When that appears to be working, they see themselves as real estate moguls. Grandiosity leads to several more transactions, and a personal guarantee of the mortgages. As real estate is cyclical, and downturns are inevitable, grandiosity often leads to bankruptcy.

Humility is required when taking out a loan. The fact that the bank will lend you $2,000,000 does not mean you want $2,000,000. Banks are just as likely as you are to forget that real estate is cyclical. Their projections may be as optimistic as yours because a larger loan portfolio means higher salaries and bonuses. Optimism and overbuilding peak at the same moment. Once tenants command and get lower rents elsewhere, your mortgage payments cannot be covered and your equity is gone. You will not be happy with real estate if your mortgage is as big as your ego.

Property type

You may be more compatible with one property type than another. Single-family homes, apartments, retail, office, existing properties, and development call for varying personality traits.

Single-family homes

Single-family homes are capital appreciation plays. Rent generally covers all expenses but not much more. However, homeowners will pay more for a home than is justified by the potential rental income. As a property owner, you must be patient and wait for a multiyear rally in home prices. Home prices can reach levels two to three times what is justified by available rents. Keep your tenant happy, but do not spend any money fixing up or improving the property. Then make cosmetic repairs just before listing. The market will do all the work for you.

Overactive investors spend too much time and money during the five to 10 years the property appreciates. Guilty investors also have trouble. They fix up the tenant's home instead of focusing on their own retirement fund. Then when it comes time to sell, they take a below-market price from their friend, the existing tenant. Some investors get so attached to the home that they never sell, living on the meager rents throughout their retirements. This is common when an owner-occupied home is converted into a rental.

Fixer-uppers

Fixer-upper investors are a different breed. These people have construction and remodeling skills. They buy homes in need of repair and remodeling, do all the work themselves, and then resell the homes at a profit. Most do this as a part-time job or hobby. Some live in the home while working on it. Overconfidence is their greatest downfall. Paying too high a price for the fixer-upper when the market peaks can lead to loss of down payment, out-of-pocket remodel expenses, and in an extreme downturn can require paying off the excess of the mortgage value over the ultimate sale price. However, many people have successfully put together large nest eggs this way and transitioned into apartments and offices. In addition to construction expertise, persistence, thriftiness, and a tolerant family are required to succeed here.

Apartments

Apartments are income generators. Activity pays off. Tenants are moving in and out all the time. You need to make cheap, lasting repairs regularly so you can always get the best rents. You need to know the neighborhood and the competition. If competitive rents drop, you need to drop rents too and keep the building 95-percent occupied. When mortgage rates drop, you want to have the papers ready to refinance.

Apartments are excellent for active personalities. They also work well for those who are good at hiring help. You must screen and supervise property managers. Limits must be set with maintenance people. Passive buy-and-hold investors will not do well with apartments. Tenants will disappear and expenses will increase.

Offices

Offices require less activity but good business evaluation skills. Leases run from three to 10 years and require tenants to pay taxes, maintenance, insurance, and other expenses. Generally, only the common areas are the responsibility of the owner.

The trick with offices is to keep long-term tenants in place. Most tenants are not Fortune 500 companies. In addition to screening your tenant's credit history, you need to assure yourself that the future of the business is sound. A business insolvency can tie up your space for months while you proceed to eviction, clean-up, and releasing.

Humility is also important in offices. Once a long lease expires, you must adjust to market rents and market realities. Wallowing in the rents you used to get does not fill empty space.

Retail

Retail property owners must be expert at selling and screening. Retail is an ever-changing world. Vacancies come quickly and unpredictably. This year's store is next year's storage bin. Long-term leases mean nothing when a tenant files for bankruptcy. You are constantly selling your property to new tenants. Yet most tenants will not stay for the long-term, even though they think they will.

Before you close a deal, you need to be sure there are very few flaws in the tenant's concept. If the flaws are too big, you have to move quickly to find other prospects and fill vacancies. You cannot wait for the right tenant to find you. You must reach out for prospects.

Active salespeople with good screening skills enjoy retail properties. Leases often contain bonus rent based on tenant gross sales. A successful tenant can be a bonanza. Introverts have difficulty with retail. Selling requires constant interaction.

Development

Development is different from buying existing buildings. Development is more than a hobby or a part-time job. Good developers work long hours. An investor will have difficulty competing.

Development is riskier than investment. Existing buildings have in-place tenants, a financial history, and a market presence. Developers must create a building as cheaply as possible and create a market for an unknown property before it is completed. Dreamers and idea people are attracted to development, as are egomaniacs. The Gillette Edmunds Tower sounds good to me.

Unfortunately, development requires more than a dream and an ego. Financing skills, land purchase talent, building supervision, marketing, leasing, and accounting talent are necessary. Though the excitement of seeing a new project rise from the ground may sustain you for a while, an overwhelming sense will soon set in for most investors.

Successful developers enjoy risk and play the odds. Development is a multiyear project. Drawing plans, securing permits, arranging financing, construction, and leasing take years. The developer must determine that future rents and occupancy levels justify current costs. Developers lured by wild projections and unsustainable up cycles fail. Realists construct game plans. They meet with zoning board members one-on-one before applying for a permit. They figure bad weather and cost overruns into the construction plan. If preleasing is poor, they shutter the project for future completion when rents and vacancies reach a specified level. Completed projects can also be closed or returned to the bank on non-recourse loans. Developers who are not comfortable with multiple contingencies are miserable. Some try to control their misery by long hours and overwork.

Development has addictive potential. Workaholics may enjoy development for a time. The excitement sustains them. But similar to all addictions, workaholism turns ugly. Your abandoned family leaves you. Lack of sleep and proper nutrition create health problems. Stress turns into yelling and depression. The market turns down and you have to give properties to the bank and lose all your equity. Suicide seems reasonable. Just remember there is help.

Most investors, though, are not workaholics.

The real estate personality

Real estate is excellent for active investors who like to tinker and those who enjoy physical interaction with their investments. Today stocks are all about blips on computer screens. Huge quantities of stock research are available free on the Web and thousands of professional analysts pour over every stock. It does not pay to visit stores and test products as it did in the early 1980s. It is not a good idea to tinker with a stock portfolio. Buy, hold, and research works best. Tinkering just runs up commissions, spreads, and taxes.

Enthusiasm is the most important element in successful real estate investing. With real estate, you can go over and cut the lawn, sweep the sidewalk, chat with the tenants, make suggestions on how they can improve their business, raise rent appropriately, refinance mortgages, hire and fire property managers and handymen. For those who like to do stuff, want active investments and active retirement, real estate is a much better fit than stocks. Day traders would be much better served cutting down expenses and taxes in their properties than running up expenses and taxes trading stocks.

Investors who have difficulty with losses do well with real estate. Successful stock investors learn to offset gains and losses. Unhappy stock investors find the pain of loss far exceeds the pleasure of gain. They hang on to their losers until the company is de-listed in a bankruptcy. Real estate, with moderate leverage, is a plodding investment. Though rents may decline in a local recession, they generally come back in the recovery and move to a higher level. Loss avoidance is a good strategy with real estate.

Investors who focus on price rather than fundamentals are better off with real estate than stocks. Real estate prices are unknown. Stock prices are quoted on TV, the Internet, newspapers, magazines, and in conversations. Accurate real estate appraisals are expensive and rarely worth doing. Real estate investors can only focus on the fundamentals, as no prices are available until a buyer makes a bona fide offer.

Real estate investment trusts (REITs)

Real estate investment trusts (REITs) are securities traded on the stock exchange. They own income-producing real estate. REITs are managed by professionals. They own large building complexes and operate in many markets.

As with real estate, REITs are considered riskier than stocks. This is primarily by those who were ripped off by the general partners of RELPs. The pain of prior losses can lead you to classify all forms of real estate as the same. In fact, REITs have fewer emotional triggers than stocks.

REIT investors experience less powerlessness than stock investors. REIT returns are less volatile than stock returns. The worst year for REITs since 1970 was negative 17 percent. The worst year for U.S. stocks was negative 26 percent. Many foreign markets have lost better than 50 percent in a year. REIT returns are negative one out of every six years. Stock returns are negative one out of every three years.

Unmanageability is also a smaller issue with REITs than with stocks. Though REIT managers are highly compensated, grant themselves stock options, and enter into mergers and acquisitions against your interest, by law they cannot control all your money. REITs are required to pay out 90 percent of earnings to shareholders. This works out to be 60 percent to 100 percent of the true profits of the company. At the worst, REIT managers can only abuse 40 percent of your money.

REITs have never been the subject of herd psychosis. The total market cap of all REITs is $150 billion. The market cap of stocks is 100 times greater. The market value of commercial real estate is about 50 times greater. REITs are relatively unknown. There is little sales pressure from family, friends, or brokers to buy REITs. In fact, investors who need attention and hype will not be happy with REITs. Cab drivers have never heard of REITs. Your brother-in-law knows all about them and is not interested.

REITs are sold individually or in mutual funds. Brokers are not much interested in REITs. Issues of churning, loads, margin accounts, and so on apply to REITs. Most often, though, brokers ignore REITs and REIT investors, as there is little volume. There are no online chat rooms, and few Web sites even mention REITs.

REIT investing is less complex than both stock and real estate investing. There are less than 400 REITs to choose from and of those, only 150 that are regularly traded. There are 10,000 stocks and countless properties. You can become a REIT expert in a year. REIT accounting and taxes are different than stock accounting but in many ways simpler. My REIT report, *REITs for the New Decade* (*www.Knexa.com*), explains everything you need to know about REITs in less than 100 pages.

REITs are easy to own. You do not have to manage properties. However, REITs can deteriorate like any investment. Losses are possible. If you refuse to sell because you want to avoid admitting mistakes and feeling regret, REITs may be troublesome.

One of the most common causes of losses is an emotional mistake by the REIT's management. Manager egos get out of hand from time to time. REITs expand too quickly through both acquisitions and development, turning a steady performer into an erratic stock. They buy trophy properties that inflate the manager's self-image and deflate your dividends. However, you do not have to fire a property manager. You need only sell the security.

Occasionally a REIT will enter into a long-lasting decline. Market conditions can ruin unlucky REITs. Many health care REITs that owned nursing homes lost more than 80 percent of their value when the federal government stopped paying rent for their tenants. You must not fall in love with REITs, avoid taking losses, or otherwise refuse to accept reality. Some of these nursing home operators went bankrupt.

At one time, REITs often took on mortgages they could not handle. That is rarely a problem now. The typical REIT has 50 percent equity in its properties. However, if your REIT increases its mortgages to more than 70 percent of real estate values, be prepared for a volatile stock price, erratic dividends, and potential losses. Highly leveraged REITs may be outside your comfort zone.

Overconfidence can affect REIT investors. Individual REITs get hot. Investors looking for ego gratification must pay attention. When the

Rockerfeller Center REIT became public in 1985, many investors wanted the prestige of owning a Rockefeller property. The REIT sellers were able to take advantage of this and got $20 a share at the IPO, an exorbitant price. Eleven years later, the troubled company was sold to private investors for $8 per share.

Sometimes overconfidence turns into grandiosity. The tech bubble sucked in both investors and REIT managers. REITs that owned tech offices and apartments in tech valleys became overpriced. REIT managers invested in and started Internet companies. REIT fund managers loaded up on tech REITs and their Internet companies. Though overall REITs had a good year in 2001, many tech-heavy REITs declined.

Being the big shot can also take hold of both individual investors and mutual fund managers. Some REIT managers become lionized. Investors want to invest with the celebrated managers. Association with a V.I.P. makes them a V.I.P. REIT mutual funds particularly make this mistake. The mutual fund managers hang out with the REIT managers at the investment conferences. Seeing how everyone is in awe of the highly recognized managers, they pay more for their REITs than is justified by the value of the assets. When you examine a REIT mutual fund, look at the fund manager's ego as well as your own.

The REIT personality type

Real estate investment trusts are not for everyone. If you are unable to buy and hold investments, do not buy REITs. Avoiding taking losses is a minor problem with REITs. Excessive trading is a bigger issue.

Often the yearly capital gain from a REIT will occur in one month or one quarter. In 2000, many REITs' entire capital gain came in the second quarter. A big quarter or a big week is never predictable. Traders have no reliable system to predict which week or quarter will be the one. What is predictable is that dividends are paid out every three months. Because half of REIT returns come from dividends, only buy-and-hold investors will benefit.

Traders often have the uncontrollable urge to do something to create returns. This will run up large commissions and spread expenses, and lead to missed dividends. This same energy applied to real estate, though, can be very beneficial. Individual properties need maintenance, repairs, marketing, accounting, refinancing, and more. Trader energy and action can improve returns on individual properties. Trading individual properties, though, is not a good idea. Six percent commissions, closing costs, and other expenses will destroy your returns.

Investors with no history of buying and holding are not likely to be able to do so with REITs; yet they may do so with real estate. However, you do not have to be an exclusive buy-and-hold type.

Many investors successfully buy and hold in some areas and trade in others. Some have sat on bonds for decades while trading stocks. Others still own their first house as a rental but routinely churn their 401(k) money. Realize that REITs are buy-and-hold money even though they trade on the stock exchanges. If you have a history of buy-and-hold with some asset classes and trading in others, you may be successful with REITs. Just don't let the fact that REITs can be traded online fool you into actually trading them online.

The biggest emotional hurdle with REITs is a sense of being out of sync with your fellow investors. Most people won't know what you are talking about when you tell them you own REITs. Others will find it boring. You must have the self-esteem to run outside the herd to be happy with REITs. Those who need the herd to push them along will not stay in REITs very long.

Corporate bonds

Have you ever bought a stock or stock fund to impress someone? You showed them that you are daring, clever, or contrary. Don't try it with corporate bonds. Bond investors get no respect. They are never fashionable like stock investors. No one at the office is likely to be interested in your bond purchases.

Bad company

Unmanageability is the main issue here. There is a big difference between corporate bonds and Treasury bonds. With Treasury bonds, both interest and principal are secure. With corporate bonds, neither interest nor principal are secure. However, for many years you will have the impression that your bonds are secure. Prices will be relatively stable. Interest payments will be made. Then suddenly your bonds have lost a quarter of their value and interest payments are in question.

Recognize that in all lending situations other than with Treasuries, you—the lender—and the company—the borrower—have opposite interests. They want to get out of paying interest and they don't want to pay back the full amount of principal.

Your interests are also opposed to those of shareholders. Unlike shareholders, lenders cannot vote on corporate policy. The right to vote is the right to alter the financial structure of the company even to the point of rendering it bankrupt and ruining your bonds. In bankruptcy, bonds have a call on the assets of the company and shareholders do not. However, shareholders can sell off or ruin all the assets before the bankruptcy occurs.

Even if there is a bankruptcy with assets, the assets may not belong to you. Bank loans generally have priority over bonds. In bankruptcy, they are paid and you get what is left. In fact, banks are in a better position than you even if the corporation staves off bankruptcy. A shaky corporation will default on its bonds before it defaults on its bank loans.

You must guard against overconfidence with corporate bonds. Corporations hire companies to rate their bonds when they sell them. They seek the highest possible ratings. High ratings mean lower interest rates and a larger issue. These ratings companies—Moody's, Standard and Poors, and Fitch—rate corporate bonds based on the information they are given by the company and their own database of research. However, corporations issue bonds at the best possible time. When the economy is strong and expansion seems logical, corporate bond issuance sets records and ratings are always high. Rating agencies forget about the last recession. Bond buyers assume the good times will continue indefinitely. Unfortunately, they won't.

Many investors trust ratings as they trust insurance companies. This kind of trust can lead to resentments and regrets. A bond rating is not an insurance policy. The agencies owe no one when they reduce investment-grade corporates to junk. When you look at rated bonds, you must realize that these are not objective ratings. These are paid estimates based primarily on selective information. Rating agencies often perform risk-consulting services for the companies they rate. This business would dry up if they rated the company's bonds too low.

Many investors want to give the rating agencies the benefit of the doubt. This form of people pleasing is also harmful. The bond market moves swiftly. Once the market realizes that a company's credit quality has deteriorated, prices decline. Rating agencies move slowly. Typically, three to six months after the price decline, ratings are changed. By then, you have lost a large chunk of principal.

Do not mistake corporate bonds for savings. Many savers think that the highest rated bonds are the equivalent to Treasury bonds. They are not. Once bonds are issued, ratings change. The higher the initial rating, the greater the possibility of downgrade, and the further the range of downgrade. Two out of every three changes are down. From 1997 through 2001, four out of every five rating changes were down. Savers in corporate bonds will have resentments and regrets.

Event risk

Bonds can shock you. The economy might be strong, interest rates steady, the company profitable, and suddenly the value of your bonds is destroyed. Corporate events, engineered by corporate management, are the cause. Corporate managers are not working for you. They are working for themselves. There are many ways they might attempt to get out of paying you your interest and principal.

Mergers and takeovers are the biggest problems. If large amounts of debt are issued in the process, you are diluted, and the price and rating of your bonds drops. Mergers and takeovers are supposed to increase synergies, improve efficiency, reduce overhead, and boost profits. This, in turn, is supposed to improve the quality of your bonds. In practice, many studies show that mergers end up in bigger pay for management, reduced profits, and lower credit quality.

Serial mergers can really ruin credit quality. Each merger can knock down the value of your bonds until they reach junk status. A bidding war for the acquired company can be a real disaster. Higher prices usually include less stock, more bonds, and more cash. However, as bondholders, you do not even get to vote on the merger. At least stockholders get to vote to ruin the company.

Stock buybacks also hurt you as they reduce cash available to repay interest and principal and are often financed with new debt. New debt must be serviced with earnings that could be used to pay your interest and retire your principal.

The grant of stock options to employees also hurts you, the bondholder. Stock options are only valuable if the price of the stock rises above the option price. If the value declines, the options are worthless, and employees will not spend money to exercise them. This gives employees an incentive to bet the company on risky ventures such as mergers, acquisitions, untested products, untested markets, untested technology, and untested corporate structures. When ventures fail, the employees still have their salaries, but your bonds are downgraded.

Attempting to control an uncontrollable situation, some bond buyers purchase lower-rated bonds in hopes the companies will be taken over by better-rated companies and the bonds upgraded. These speculations do not always work out. Often, lower-rated investment grade bonds turn into junk.

Discounted bonds are another strategy to control the uncontrollable. Discounted bonds sell at less than face value. For example, a $10,000 bond might sell for $8,000. Sensing a bargain, you may be lured out of your comfort zone. The upside is limited to the face value of bonds plus the interest payments. The downside is loss of all principal and interest.

Discounted bonds are discounted for a reason, often that the company is running out of cash. In order to raise cash, the company will likely sell junk bonds. Now required to pay interest on your bonds and on the junk bonds, your discounted bonds turn into junk as well. Most attempts to control the uncontrollable lead you outside your comfort zone.

Market issues lead to tissues

You are powerless over the market price of bonds as well as unable to control corporate actions. Moreover, there is no financial benefit to be derived by market movements. Your $10,000, 10-year, 7-percent bond has a high value when 10-year rates are 5 percent and a low value when 10-year rates are 9 percent. If you sell when rates are 5 percent, you will get more than $10,000, but will only be able to reinvest at 5 percent. If you sell when rates are 9 percent, you will get less than $10,000, but you can reinvest at 9 percent. No matter which direction interest rates move, you cannot benefit by trading bonds.

Overconfidence may cause you to attempt to beat this system. You sell when the price of your bond rises and hold cash until prices come down again. After all, corporate bond prices are volatile. Your optimistic brain will label this as opportunity. It is not. Innumerable studies show that interest rates cannot be predicted. While you sit on cash, prices may continue to rise indefinitely. Even if prices decline, you have paid commissions and spreads on both sides of the transaction.

Large price swings make corporate bonds inappropriate for many investors. Corporate bond prices are as volatile as stocks with lower returns. Longer durations have wilder price swings than short durations, but even five-year bonds can move up and down 20 percent in a few months. Many forces contribute to the wild price swings. The Federal Reserve tries to cool an overheated economy, as it did in 1994 and 1999, and you lose a third of your value. Bond market vigilantes also knock prices around dramatically. The vigilantes run huge pension and insurance company portfolios.

They are inflation paranoid and are also obsessed with bond supply, recessions, and other obscurities that destroy the price of your bonds.

Bond funds

Bond fund managers believe they can predict interest rates. However, they make their living on salary, not bond returns. Bond fund managers are highly paid, averaging more than $375,000 a year in 2001. Their salaries continue to rise despite poor results. Trading bonds will not break their egos. They feel the necessity to do something to justify a big salary. You would be better off if they did nothing but collect interest and reinvest maturing principal. Their overconfidence and high salaries cost you dearly.

Overconfidence leads to trading. Trading incurs spreads and commissions. Some managers simply trade into cash and wait. Cash returns less than bonds but it keeps the fund price steady. Steady funds lose few investors. Eventually they trade back into bonds, costing more spreads and commissions.

Overconfidence can turn into grandiosity. Grandiose fund managers borrow money against the fund assets to buy more bonds. The borrowed money must be repaid with interest. Unfortunately, when the quality of the bond portfolio deteriorates, there will be no interest to keep the debt current, so your principal will have to be used to pay off the debt.

Grandiose managers also believe they can buy lower-quality issues to increase reported yield without suffering consequences. Higher yield keeps investors in the fund. Unfortunately, at the first economic slow down, low-quality issues turn into junk and NAV declines.

You may believe that you can pick quality managers. This overconfidence can hurt you. Most bond fund managers are more concerned with asset gathering and their high salaries than returns.

This may lead you to bond index funds. Index funds are, of course, the ultimate asset gatherers. Unfortunately, bond index funds have problems. Bond index funds have high turnover, often as much as 50 percent a year, because bond indexes change all the time. High turnover causes high expenses and high taxes. Still, index funds outperform 60 percent of bond funds.

Some investors turn to closed-end bond funds. CEFs can be found that sell at steep discounts to net asset value and high yields. Unfortunately, management grandiosity is even worse with CEFs than with open-end funds. Because shareholders cannot redeem and reduce assets under management, CEF managers get into leverage, junk, foreign bonds, convertibles, and more.

Bonding with bonds

Few investors are comfortable with corporate bonds. Trading, moving in and out of different qualities, predicting interest rates, raising cash, and all other active strategies only reduce returns. To be a happy bond buyer, you must hold quality issues until maturity and then reinvest at existing rates. You must be able to accept a decade of wild swings in price and credit quality without buying or selling. Despite dramatic ups and downs in price and ratings, more than 98 percent of investment-grade bonds mature without a hitch. Sitting and doing nothing is the trick. You must be able to process your feelings without taking action. Reacting to downgrades costs money. Prices always decline substantially before the downgrade is issued. Reacting to interest rates is equally harmful. Commissions and spreads are costly, yet the direction of interest rates can change at any time. Humility is required. Going to cash, leveraging the account, and believing you can out-guess credit ratings all will lead to anxiety, regrets, and depression.

Oil and gas

Stocks are pieces of paper or computer blips that only have value if other investors are willing to pay for them. When stocks are out of fashion, there may be no profits for decades. Stock prices were flat from 1966–1982. Oil and gas are highly useful commodities. Once extracted from the ground, they can always be sold. Even when the price of oil is too low to cover the costs of production, oil in the ground has value as an option on future production. As oil prices fluctuate, there is always hope a time will come when the market price justifies the cost of extraction.

How limited is your partnership

Relationship issues dominate oil and gas investing. Oil and gas deals are usually limited partnerships. You are buying a relationship with the general partners. You may find the partnership on your own or you may find it through a broker. This leads to relationship issues with the broker.

Broker issues are similar to those with other investments. People pleasing can lead you to buy deals that are not appropriate for you. Brokers receive large commissions for selling limited partnerships. Each partnership has its own commission structure. The broker wants to sell you the largest amount of the highest commission product.

Your broker will tell you something very different. He will tell you that you are in an exclusive class of upper echelon investors who have the privilege of investing in this rare offering. Your ego may tell you he is right, you are smart about brokers and oil and gas, and you have the bank account to prove it. The fact that you know nothing about brokers or oil and gas is not a deterrent to your ego. Overconfidence can cost you money here.

Once you have purchased the deal, the good news is there is little churning, as there is little secondary market for your interests once you buy them. The bad news is, you may feel trapped. Even if the deal is a good one, but you need the money for something else, you are stuck. Also, as a limited partner, you have no rights to control or change most aspects of the deal.

If you are able to evaluate the deal objectively before you buy, you will have to deal with confusion, complexity, and trust. There are many types of oil and gas deals. The most common types are drilling, income, royalty, completion, and lease acquisition. Within each type, there are different expense structures, tax implications, and probabilities of success. The unknowns include the amount of oil in the ground, the quality, the cost of production, and the market price during production. The general partners will make estimates of as many factors as possible, but you will have to judge their ability to estimate and their experience. Most of your information will come from a prospectus. This document is written in unintelligible legalese.

Overconfidence can hurt you in these deals if it leads you to trust untrustworthy general partners. Though everything looks fine on paper and your broker urges you to buy, you need to pay close attention to the general partners' track record with public partnerships. You need to interview other investors who have invested with these general partners. You must eliminate partnerships that are knowingly sold by general partners with little prospect of success. These deals gather information for their future private deals. The best way to find the location of oil under the ground is to drill wells. Each well leads you closer to the center of the field. General partners sometimes sell limited partnerships to finance test wells. Once they know where the oil is located, they drill the producing wells themselves and keep all the production.

Choose your areas of powerlessness

If you feel comfortable with brokers and general partners, then you get to choose the type of deal within your comfort zone. Each type of deal entails different areas of powerlessness and unmanageability:

◆ Royalty funds buy the right to receive a fixed percentage of the gross production of producing wells. You are buying oil without regard to the expenses of production. While it is a certainty that the wells are producing, you are powerless over the price of oil and gas and the life of the wells. Wells can produce for 20 or more years or only a few months. The price of oil in the last five years has been as low as $10 a barrel and as high as $35 a barrel. Also, as production is already underway, there is no possibility the wells will suddenly become gushers.

◆ Income funds invest in producing oil and gas deals. Deals include both revenue and expenses. Income funds receive a higher percentage of gross production than royalty funds, but they are responsible to pay operating costs. In addition to the risks of price and duration of the well, you also bear the risk that the operators of the well can make repairs, replacements, and workovers efficiently. In most deals, the cost of drilling and production can be estimated based on the costs of other wells in the area. If the price of oil declines substantially, both income funds and royalty funds may stop producing. However, there is still value in your investment. You have the option to produce when prices rise. Whereas stocks can be in a 15-year slump because their only productive use, raising capital for business, can be done through bank loans, bonds, and profit retention, oil and gas has no current substitute. It is needed to keep the economy functioning. Eventually demand and prices pick up.

◆ Completion funds invest in discovered oil and gas that has not yet been produced. In addition to the risks of income funds, you do not know the exact quantity of oil and gas that can be produced nor the exact cost of bringing it to the surface. However, you receive a higher percentage of revenue than either a royalty fund or an income fund. Most completion funds involve wells that have never been produced. Horizontal drilling funds use wells that have already produced. In these deals, existing wells are redrilled from the bottom of the well horizontally into the reservoir. Typically these deal produce large quantities of oil for short periods of time, often as little as a year. The risk is whether or not the costs of drilling will be covered by the payout.

◆ A drilling fund involves all the risks of the other funds as well as the risk that you will drill a dry hole. Most funds drill several prospects to mitigate the risks. If you hit a gusher, you can make huge profits. But a series of dry holes is also possible as well as a series of uneconomic discoveries.

Some investors are comfortable with a variety of deals. For others, even royalty funds are outside their comfort zone. Fortunately, there are still other investments to consider.

Other investments

During the past century, many forms of investments have become common.

Zero coupon bonds

These bonds pay no interest. Instead, they are sold at a discount from face value. At maturity, you are paid face value. For example, in 2001 a 30-year treasury zero sold for $20,000. In 2031, it will mature at $100,000.

Zeros work for certain personalities, as they trigger both a sense of powerlessness and a sense of control.

You are powerless over the price of zeros before maturity. Zeros are more volatile than regular bonds as interest is not paid currently. In fact, zeros are the most volatile of all bonds with similar maturity and credit quality. When rates rise, they will take the biggest losses. When rates decline, they are the biggest gainers. As interest rates are not predictable, many investors are not compatible with zeros.

Zeros also entail unmanageability. Commissions and spreads are high on the purchase of most zeros. Shopping for better deals is tricky. You encounter mathematical complexity as you must calculate imputed interest on older issues in order to make comparisons.

Funds, known as target maturity funds, are available. The fund managers make the calculations for you. However, the funds have loads and expenses and sometimes trade zeros to your detriment.

Tax issues are annoying. The IRS taxes imputed income, the amount of appreciation toward face value that occurs each year. You get no cash but must pay taxes out of pocket on this imputed income. Zeros in IRAs and 401(k)s avoid this issue.

Corporate zeros are only for those who can accept an extreme degree of powerlessness. Credit risk is high for zeros that are not Treasuries. With standard corporate bonds, current interest compensates for risk of future defaults. Some bond investors calculate how long it takes to get their money back through interest and then how much profit they will get from future interest payments and at maturity. For example, they calculate that a $10,000, 30-year bond pays $800 a year in interest; after 12 1/2 years interest totals $10,000; thereafter, all interest payments and the principal payment at maturity are profit. With zeros, you get neither interest nor principal until maturity. If the corporation goes under before maturity, you may get nothing from your investment.

Treasury zeros offer a sense of predictability for investors who can truly ignore market fluctuations until maturity. Long-term zeros eliminate the issue of reinvestment as well. Every time a bond matures, bond investors can only reinvest at the current interest rates. If interest rates are high, this is a good thing. But if interest rates are low, this is a problem. A 30-year zero eliminates this issue for 30 years. However, long zeros lock in an imputed rate until maturity. You must be able to accept this imputed rate for the entire term.

Treasury zeros are one of the few truly buy and ignore investments. However, if you cannot ignore them, you should avoid them. There is plenty to worry about and nothing that can be done. Your locked-in interest rate may not keep up with inflation. Prices may drop below your cost for a period of years. Trading into other zeros incurs commissions and spreads but does not improve returns. Ignoring price fluctuations is mandatory. If you obsess on prices, zeros are not for you.

Convertible bonds

Convertible bonds are a hybrid of stocks and bonds. Similar to bonds, they pay fixed interest and have a maturity date. However, in exchange for a lower interest rate and a longer maturity than offered on the company's standard bonds, you are given the right to convert your bonds into stock if the stock price rises to a set level. This option to convert has value even though the current stock price is lower than the conversion price. As stock prices fluctuate wildly, you could hit the conversion price at any time. Meanwhile, you collect interest, which is higher than the dividend yield on the stock. Once the convert is in the money, you do not have to convert. You can continue to collect interest and convert at any time before maturity.

Complexity is rampant with converts. The scenario just described is the most common. However, converts can include zero coupons, calls, puts, fluctuating conversion prices, contingent conversion prices, fluctuating interest rates, merger and acquisition provisions, and more. Tax issues are beyond description.

Powerlessness and unmanageability are everywhere. The price fluctuates with both the price of the stock and the price of bonds, as well as interest rates and the economy. Converts are marketed as less volatile than stocks because they pay interest and mature at face value. In practice, converts are just as volatile as stocks. Most converts are issued by low quality companies; neither interest payments nor principal are secure.

Overconfidence is the biggest issue with converts. You will imagine the stock price soaring and you will believe you are being paid a nice rate of interest while you wait to cash in your huge capital gain. Neither is likely to happen.

Broker issues are difficult with convertible bonds. People pleasing will hurt you here. Spreads and commissions are high. Converts trade rarely. Some become illiquid. There are about $180 billion in converts versus $1.5 trillion of investment-grade debt. When brokers cannot sell you stocks because the market is bad, they invent their own converts. Often the convert is a AAA bond that can be converted into an index fund such as a NASDAQ fund. For investors burned by stocks, the enticement is a secure bond with a chance for stock-like gains. Unfortunately, these have huge commissions. The commissions and spreads will absorb 10 percent of your capital. Also, the AAA bond will pay half or less of the current interest on AAA bonds. Worst of all, you will only be able to convert into the index fund when the index is highly overvalued and set for a big fall.

If you have had a poor experience with stock mutual funds, your mutual fund family may offer you convertible bond funds instead. Convertible bond mutual funds are marketed as more secure than stock mutual funds. Unlike stock mutual funds, they have a yield and maturity. In practice, management fees eat up most of the yield and low quality creates both volatility and unsatisfactory returns. Overconfident and grandiose managers lose money trading and buying IPO converts.

Few investors are happy with converts. Overconfidence is the biggest problem. Most investors are suckered into converts by the lure of secure interest and principal with a seemingly free stock option. When the convert is busted by management and the market, they are deeply disappointed.

The happy convert investor knows he does not know. He does extensive research and usually buys already busted converts. He diversifies but trades less than once a year. Few investors have the humility and patience to do well with converts.

Ginnie Maes

Ginnie Maes are mutual funds that own pools of home mortgages. These are not savings instruments. Interest and principal are at risk.

You may experience powerlessness with Ginnie Maes. You lose value both when rates rise and when they decline. When rates decline, homeowners refinance. You get your principal back and can only reinvest in mortgages that pay the new, lower rates. When rates rise, your interest is fixed because no one refinances their home at higher rates. However, the value of your principal now declines. Your $100,000 that pays 7 percent is less valuable than the $100,000 mortgages that pay 9 percent.

Unmanageability is also an issue with Ginnie Maes. Management fees eat into returns. Trading incurs commissions and spreads. Management strategies backfire.

To avoid prepayments, managers buy discounted mortgages. For example, discount mortgages that pay 7 percent are available when current rates are 9 percent. Prepayment risk is reduced as few people refinance 7-percent mortgages at 9 percent. However, interest rates are not predictable. When rates rise, the value of discounted mortgages is lacerated.

Managers also invest in lower quality, higher coupon mortgages that are rarely refinanced like mobile home loans. Fees and expenses of refinancing mobile homes are too high to make refinancing worthwhile. This strategy may increase returns for a period of time, but it eventually backfires. Mobile homes often depreciate in value over time. In a recession, many mobile home loans default, but the value of the home does not cover the principal remaining on the mortgage.

Ginnie Mae fund managers may suffer from an inability to do nothing for their huge salaries.

Investors with low expectations are comfortable with Ginnie Maes. Volatility is less than with stocks but higher than with most savings instruments. Returns are better than from savings instruments and slightly more predictable than stock returns. Savers who mistake Ginnie Maes as savings instruments become uncomfortable, because both interest and principal fluctuate.

Tax lien certificates

Enterprising investors have many options that are not available to passive investors. Tax lien certificates (TLCs) are one of these options. Relative to stocks, TLCs offer more manageability and predictability, and there never will be a herd of investors messing with TLC prices.

When property taxes are delinquent, counties impose a lien on the property for the amount of tax due plus any penalties and interest. Then the county proceeds to collect. Collection can take many years, while counties need money right away. In many states, counties are allowed to sell these liens at auction so they can get some cash in their coffers immediately. These liens, known as tax lien certificates, can be purchased at auction at substantial discounts to face value or in some states at fixed discounts. Enterprising investors travel around the country to attend auctions and buy TLCs.

TLCs have several advantages. They are not sold by brokers, insurance salespeople, or anyone looking for commissions or spreads. People pleasers have no worries here. TLCs have secure features. Tax liens have priority over mortgage liens, IRS liens, and almost all other liens.

However, there are several areas of powerlessness and unmanageability:

◆ You will not know in advance when you will collect your principal and interest. Counties try to collect on your behalf for a few years, but if they fail, you must hire an attorney and foreclose on the property. The whole process could take five years.

◆ Returns are variable. If you bid poorly, returns may be low. If you foreclose and there are few other liens on the property, returns could be enormous.

◆ Some properties turn out to be worth less than the lien. A fire may have destroyed the building but the owner had no fire insurance, yet the land is worth less than the cost of removing the rubble. Or environmental clean-up of the property costs more than its value. Land in a flood plain where flood insurance is no longer available is worthless.

◆ Foreclosure has costs. Lawyers and court fees must be paid. While most states require the property owner to pay your legal cost in a foreclosure, the property may not have enough value to cover all these costs and the owner may be bankrupt. In some situations, the owner's bankruptcy can destroy the value of the lien. In bankruptcy, the bankruptcy judge controls the property. The lien may be dismissed or given only partial payment if administrative costs exceed the value of all property.

◆ Even successful foreclosure requires substantial time and attention. After foreclosure, the property must either be sold or held and managed. Adding up all hours spent and profits made may result in little profit per hour.

Overconfidence can hurt you here. TLCs have risks. High rates of interest are available when owners are simply delinquent and redeem liens once the county has sent out notices. But you must investigate the owner and the property to determine the likelihood of redemption. Investors looking for big gains through foreclosure must be certain that the property has value and the owner will not be able to redeem the lien. Passive investors will not be happy here.

Active investors have fun with TLCs. They travel from state to state, vacation most of the time, and spend a few days at the courthouse and around the property. Some build substantial real estate portfolios from foreclosures. Others relish high returns without ever staring at a computer screen or sitting in a brokerage office. However, for those who enjoy being in the herd, TLCs feel too isolated and independent.

Enterprising investors will also find more options in the next chapter.

CHAPTER 6

SPECULATIONS

*A*s you read this chapter, consider if you are compatible with speculation. Speculation triggers different emotions than saving or investing. Consider which specific speculations may be within your comfort zone. When you reach Step 3, which involves matching investments and your personality, you will return to Step 1 to find compatible investments. Some of you will want speculations for part of your portfolio.

Speculation is any investment in assets with unpredictable returns over both the short-term and the long-term. There are no sure systems to do well with speculations. Ideally, speculation is funded with cash that is not needed for savings or investment.

Not all readers need to study this chapter. After reading the following section, you might wish to look only at the sections on speculations you now own or have owned in the past. Then, those of you who have a strong sense that you are a speculator should study the entire chapter. Those who are confident that speculations are not within your comfort zone should skip the rest of the chapter. If you are not sure, skim the rest of the chapter.

Speculators use magical belief systems

The rationale and belief systems employed by speculators vary widely. Most speculators believe in their own genius and ingenuity. With genius and ingenuity, they develop systems. The systems use mathematics, charts, patterns, and randomness. Day traders, options players, and commodity purchasers usually employ their own systems.

Other speculators believe gods, luck, or higher powers will deliver great profits with little work. Many gamble on a feeling rather than any research. Others think their magic power resides in their ability to exploit errors of other speculators, rather than any developed system.

Speculation is often a lonely game. The successful speculator credits his genius or personal channel to a higher power. When speculation fails, there is no one to blame but the speculator. Speculation is about the relationship with one's self. In the extremes, losing all can lead to self-loathing and self-destructive acts; winning millions can lead to self-adoration and egomania.

Internal balance is the key to successful speculation. The mental processes can be confusing, distorting, and cause irrational behavior. The speculator is a lone individual trying to beat the odds in a small, closed system.

Options

For the right speculator, options are fun.

Stock options are the right to buy or sell a fixed number of shares of a specified stock for a fixed, short-term period.

Long-term stock returns are reasonably predictable. Options are only available for the short-term. Short-term stock returns are unpredictable. For savers and investors, unpredictability is to be avoided. For speculators, unpredictable short-term returns are the challenge.

Some option players love complex strategies. Others enjoy the mathematics. Valuing options requires advanced mathematics. Many players ignore the math and play hunches. The real fun is to combine buys, sells, puts, calls, longs, shorts, durations, individual options and index futures, multiple contracts, margin, and multiple securities to cover all the angles. If you dislike complexity, you will not enjoy this.

Speculators who take speculation too seriously are unhappy. Option players get into emotional trouble when they start to believe they can beat the system. Options are a closed system. For every buyer, there is a seller.

Options are expiring contracts that are bought and sold. Unlike stocks or real estate, they have no intrinsic value that can grow with the economy. While some players beat the system, as a whole, no one wins; in fact, expenses ensure that there are more losers than winners. Option expenses are high and continuous. Commissions are charged when you purchase and when you exercise or assign the option. As options expire or are exercised, new options must be purchased and then exercised or assigned. The longer you play, the more expensive it is.

New players need to learn to say no to their brokers. People pleasing can lead to high expenses. Brokers encourage complex strategies. They call owning a single option "naked." True speculators sometimes find running around naked fun. Tentative speculators don't want to go around naked; they cover up with offsetting options. Using a spread, long positions are offset by short positions.

Brokers have charming names for all the systems they sell: straddles, spreads, strangles, married puts. Each system requires multiple options, which incur additional commissions and spreads and expire or are exercised and must be renewed. These strategies are supposed to let you sleep at night as all risks are covered. However, your broker is partying on your money while you are sleeping. Once you wake up and add up all the expenses, you must determine if this kind of fun is within your budget and your comfort zone.

Brokers will argue that these strategies put options in your comfort zone. The truth is that strategies can be devised that take the volatility out of your investments. Instead, you simply incur a slow, steady erosion of capital as you pay commissions and incur spreads until one day all your capital is gone. Your good night's sleep turns into a coma.

Option sellers appeal to your ego. They devise beginner, intermediate, and advanced strategies. Ambitious speculators want to move up the scale quickly. This can be expensive. Private option advisories sell newsletters, hotlines, and seminars. Private advisory services are expensive, have deceptive track records, and make money from their fees whether or not you profit from their strategies. Often the record of accomplishment is based on hypothetical trading or the one of many accounts that showed profits. Brokers provide options reports written by their derivatives' gurus. Brokerage advice is free, though trades are certainly not free.

Options players often have a sense of free-floating fear. Your strategies appear successful, but you have a sense of impending doom. Focusing on the small details of your strategies and not looking at the big picture causes the free-floating fear. For example, covered strategies often end in many small losses, a few small gains, and an occasional big hit. This encourages you, often for years. Every month you buy new positions with part of your salary and the proceeds from your closed positions. But your subconscious realizes that a series of small losses is the equivalent of one large loss. And while you keep excellent records as to what strategies are working and what are not, you have not calculated the return on your invested capital. In fact, you have probably lost more than half your capital.

Focusing on the big picture—long term you are certain to lose money—causes unwavering fear.

One option is a treatment center

Addiction is an issue for option players. Because high costs stack the deck against you, for many players, the longer you play, the larger your losses. But addicts do not see it that way. The longer they play, the better chance of making that big score.

You must look for the symptoms of addiction. Are you thinking about options when you are at work or with family? After your margin account was called, did you take out credit card loans, a second mortgage, or borrow from friends to keep playing? Though once happy playing options, are you now unhappy or numb? If any of this is close to home, visit Gambler's Anonymous for a few meetings.

Stock investors get sucked into the options game. Though you realize you are powerless over market movements, fear may lead you to try to control the market. Fear combined with people pleasing can turn you into a speculator.

In a bear market, your broker will recommend that you protect the value of your portfolio from further declines by buying puts. In a bull market, she advises you that you can increase your returns with calls. In a slow market, you can generate some income by selling calls and collecting premiums. After rallies, you can insure your gains buying puts. After dips, you can bet on a rally with calls. Once you take the bait, the market may go against your puts or calls. You are then advised of further strategies to cover your puts, calls, and stocks. In a matter of months, you may find yourself an options expert and much poorer for it.

The happy options player accepts the odds of loss and plays for the fun of playing. Inadvertent options players are miserable.

Employer stock options

The bull market of the 1990s turned many employees into inadvertent options players. Most employees are savers and investors. Being compensated for work with a speculation is troubling.

Once vested, employee stock options allow employees to buy a fixed number of shares at a fixed strike price for a fixed period.

Some executives negotiate for stock options instead of cash. Overconfidence and even grandiosity engendered from high salaries and a high position trigger a belief that they can determine the direction of their company's stock. The strike price is set above the stock price at the time the options are issued. When the stock price soars above the strike price, options are very valuable. However, anytime the stock price drops below the strike price, the value disappears. Unfortunately, overconfidence often turns into disappointment.

Employees who accept options in lieu of cash exchange certainty for powerlessness. Sometimes during the vesting period, the price of the stock stays below the strike price and the options expire worthless. For overpriced stocks, a return to real value can leave the price below the strike price for a decade.

Even when options vest in the money, problems of manageability surface. There are two common strategies to exercise. One is borrow, buy the shares, sell shares to pay the loan and taxes, and sit on remaining shares. Here, only the future stock price is a source of unmanageability.

The grandiose exercise method is borrow, buy and hold all shares, and pay no taxes or loan principal until at least April 15 of the following year to take full advantage of the certain continuing climb of the stock price. Here, the stock price, the loan interest and principal payments, and the taxes are all sources of unmanageability. Yet many executives use this method of exercise.

Having seen the stock price rise above the strike price and keep on climbing, overconfidence sets in. These executives truly believe that the stock price will continue to rise. Surrounded at work by others with the same belief and the same loyalty to the company, overconfidence turns into grandiosity. Grandiosity then says maximize the gain by holding all shares; there is no need to hedge against a decline and pay the taxes and loan early. As volatile companies issue most stock options, many executives have seen the stock crash, leaving them with no money to pay taxes and loan principal.

Once executives believe that stock options are better than cash, they leave themselves open for the worst experiences of speculators. Sometimes selling the stock after exercise is restricted for a period of time. To get some benefit during the lock-up period, many executives take out loans against the value of the stocks. Then the stocks crash, but the loans need to be paid. Or an executive buys a fixer-upper mansion with a loan against the restricted stock and a huge mortgage. At the same time as the stock crashes, the market for mansions crashes, and the executive then loses the house and the stock but is left with a loan to pay.

Tax issues are complex and hurt overconfident executives. With most plans, when you exercise your options you must pay taxes on the profits at the highest rates. Some schemes trigger enormous alternative minimum taxes. In many cases, employees have no knowledge that taxes are due other than what has been withheld from their paychecks. When April 15 arrives, they are stuck with a huge tax liability. If the stock price has collapsed, they have no capital to pay the taxes.

Ignorant of the volatility of stock prices, companies attempt to mitigate losses for employees. This compounds the emotional issues. For tax reasons, rather than reprice existing options, companies give employees the right to cancel them and receive new options six months and a day later. Employees must then decide if they want to bet the stock price does or does not recover over the next six months. If they agree to take new options, they have six months of not knowing either the stock price or the option price. During the waiting period, employees have incentive to hurt the stock price so options will be cheap when reissued. After the six months, they are back to the usual powerlessness and unmanageability of owning stock options. If the stock price soared during the wait, the option price will be high and may be a set-up for another crash in the stock.

Few executives are happy speculators. More than half the options issued in the late 1990s expired worthless. Though overconfidence and even grandiosity initiate executives into stock option schemes, most executives I have worked with avoid option packages when searching for the next job.

Debt instruments

Most investors think of bonds as savings or investments. However, many forms of bonds are only appropriate for speculators.

Junk bonds

Junk bonds are corporate bonds with low credit ratings and high yields. Junk bonds are often mistaken for investments rather than speculations.

Speculators understand the risks. These include downside and upside risks. The downside includes loss of both principal and interest.

In any five- to 10-year economic cycle, 10 percent or more of junk bonds default. In 1991 alone, 13 percent defaulted. Many other junk bonds will decline by half or more. High yields are not what they seem. Though yields average 11 percent, this is misleading. Every time a junk bonds defaults, it is taken out of the average. Average yields are based solely on the survivors.

There are also risks on the upside. Most junk bonds are callable. If the corporation issuing them is successful, then they will redeem your bonds and end your high returns. Once a bond is called, you must speculate again in a new bond.

The speculator must balance the risk of default with the risk of call. Often within a few years of issuance, either occurs. Time is a big factor. Speculators must collect as much interest as they can as quickly as they can, as well as play for quick capital gains and then get out. This is challenging.

Junk bonds have high volatility. Prices are determined by herd psychosis. Markets are dominated by mutual funds and flow in and out of mutual funds. When junk funds are popular and flows into funds increase, prices soar. When unpopular, prices are destroyed.

The height of popularity occurs when the economy is peaking and growth prospects appear unlimited. This is when the worst credits can sell junk bonds. After the peak, the economy slows down, bonds default, and no one wants the survivors at any price. In the late 1980s, many leveraged buy-out junk bonds defaulted. Recently, telecom and tech junk bonds defaulted en mass.

Overconfidence is the biggest issue for speculators. Overconfidence will tell you that you have the ability to outguess the market.

Investors and savers are sometimes sold junk bonds as high yield savings or investments. Wishful thinking, lack of research, succumbing to a sales pitch, or gullibility can all cause savers and investors to speculate in junk bonds. Greed is occasionally a factor as well.

Savers are particularly hurt when they discover what they have purchased. Many think they have purchased something secure such as a Treasury bond. In fact, they have the opposite. In a recession, Treasuries do well; junk bonds turn into trash.

Investors often get into junk through mutual funds. While it would be clear to you that an individual junk bond is a speculation, you can rationalize that owning a diversified group of them managed by a professional makes them an investment. Overconfidence is a factor. While you concede that you cannot pick junk bonds, you believe you have the ability to pick mutual fund managers who can outguess the market. In fact, mutual funds are terrible with junk bonds. Many junk bond funds have lost more than half their value since they first became popular in the late 1980s.

Mutual fund families often try to pass off their junk bond funds as something other than speculations. High yields are emphasized as mitigating risk. In fact, defaults cut not only the net asset value of the fund but yield, as defaulted issues yield nothing.

Mutual fund managers' overconfidence can hurt you. Recently, mutual fund managers were buying busted convertibles with yields as high as 50 percent a year. These are even more volatile than new junk issues. The speculation was that interest would be paid long enough to cover both the investment and a profit or that these things will mature at par for a huge gain. Unfortunately, many went bankrupt before any profit was realized.

Closed-end junk funds are for pure speculators. They are even more volatile than open-end funds as discounts can widen at the same time NAV declines.

Junk notes

Some speculations, including junk notes, are marketed only to savers and investors. Savers and investors, impatient with modest returns, are often conned into buying junk notes.

Admitted speculators are too cynical to purchase junk notes; they always look for a way out. They want to either take profits or losses and move on so they can keep playing the game. Junk notes cannot be sold once you purchase them.

Junk notes come in many forms, all disguised. None carry the label "junk." Many businesses lack capital. Banks lend primarily to known quality businesses. Low-quality businesses must raise money from unsophisticated savers and investors. Risky businesses are very creative; they manage to foist junk notes onto the public.

Junk notes have terms from 18 months to 60 months. They are issued by less secure credits than junk bonds. A 10-year junk bond issuer must at least convince somebody that it will be around for 10 years. To sell an 18-month junk note, the issuer only needs to show viability for 18 months.

Your greed will be used against you here. Junk notes promise high interest on seemingly secure short-term notes, but they are tremendous products for the sellers, not for you. Commissions and spreads can be as high has 25 percent. Upon purchase, your principal will immediately be severed. Yet these are always marketed as safe, high-yielding, short-term investments. They are presented similarly to CDs, only they pay interest rates of 12 percent to 60 percent. If that 60 percent caught your eye, it may have also caught your greed.

For example, promising returns greater than 40 percent, you can invest in accounts receivables sold off by distressed companies. Of course, you do not buy them directly. You buy them through a broker, who takes a big cut of your cash, passes the rest off to the distressed seller, and leaves you with potentially worthless accounts receivables.

If it sounds too good to be true, is it just good enough for you?

Terminology will suck you in. Junk notes have secure-sounding names: prime rate certificates, investment notes, accounts receivable certificates, secured investment contracts. However, none of these things are secure, prime, certified, or even investments.

Prime rate funds are particularly deceptive. Low-credit borrowers often approach banks for large sums. Rather than lend the entire sum, a bank will lead a small portion and form a group to lend the excess. Prime rate funds are mutual funds that specialize in lending the excess sums to the banks' riskiest borrowers. Savers buy shares in the fund because of the high interest rates and because the name implies the borrowers are prime rate customers of banks. In fact, the borrowers are the worst customers of the banks. Savers, believing that principal is fixed, soon discover that principal erodes quickly. And as with junk bond funds, shocks are in store. Prime rate funds often value their junk at cost until it becomes worthless and the SEC forces them to write it off.

Impulse buyers need to beware here of one of the most common gimmicks. Junk notes, junk note funds, junk bonds, and even some corporate bonds are sold over the telephone using high-pressure tactics. All the wonderful attributes of the note will be described to you, but before you have time to ask questions, you will be told that this terrific offer must be purchased immediately or it will disappear; buyers are lining up and you have been chosen to receive the last allotment. The lure of outsmarting the other investors may be too much for you. Resentment and regret are built in for those who take the leap.

Some savers invest in these things knowing they will take losses. It is apparent to almost anyone that a 40-percent return is too good to be true. Bad investing is sometimes a cover for self-destruction. Some investors believe they need to get rid of their money but cannot give it away. Instead, they embark on a path of speculation in order to eliminate all their funds under the guise of attempting to make profits. This pattern is possible with all speculations.

Foreign and emerging market bonds

Foreign and emerging market bonds are another asset class that has completely unpredictable returns for U.S. investors. Returns on non-U.S. bonds are determined by the value of the dollar, non-U.S. interest rates, non-U.S. economics, and non-U.S. capital flows into and out of bonds. None of these factors is predictable short term and most are only loosely predictable long term. In combination, they cannot be predicted either way.

Speculators can have fun here. They can speculate on many factors: trade, international politics, government defaults, Japanese deflation, Brazilian inflation, the International Monetary Fund, the World Bank, rating changes, savings rates, bank failures, and the collapse of currency exchange systems. International romance and intrigue are the side benefits of investing abroad.

Most individuals speculate through mutual funds. You must not succumb to mutual fund pitches that imply these bond funds are for savers or investors. Their principal and interest are always in flux due to exchange rate changes. They cannot be counted in a U.S. deflation, inflation, recession, or expansion.

Many mutual funds hedge currencies to reduce the dollar risk. Nevertheless, they do not end up with the equivalent of U.S. bonds. The cost of hedging is high and the quality of foreign bonds is low, and the mutual fund expenses are so high that you end up with low interest junk bonds.

The mutual fund pitch to investors is that diversification into many different countries mitigates the risk. It does not. Herd psychosis is widespread here. When the Russian government defaulted on its debt in 1998, it affected every market. The Mexican panic of 1994 spread everywhere. In every major debt crisis, all the professionals panicked together, at the bottom. Only those comfortable with speculation will enjoy non-U.S. bonds.

Trust deeds

Trust deed come in two general categories. Some are loans to property developers secured by unfinished buildings. Others are second or third mortgages secured against existing buildings. Trust deeds are sold individually and in packages. All offer very high interest rates.

The major emotional issue is gullibility. Promoters are selling a speculation as an investment. Your overconfidence may entice you to believe that a lien on a building will protect you. The promoters will encourage that belief. They will also offer you a package of several deals for diversification. They will show you how the risk is only short-term, 18 to 24 months. They will sometimes guarantee the return of your principal.

In fact, these are pure speculations. Short-term means nothing. No one can predict when a borrower will go under or a real estate recession will begin. There is a reason someone takes out a second or third mortgage or has to find construction financing outside normal lending practices. Are you willing to speculate that you know what that reason is, that all the other lenders were wrong to deny financing, and that your principal is covered if things do not work out?

Trust deeds often pay interest of 12 percent to 14 percent to you, but remember: the promoter is also getting a big percentage. Are you willing to speculate that the borrower can afford 20 percent or higher interest and that the property is valuable enough in foreclosure to cover all the mortgages, interest, and foreclosure expenses? In real estate downturns, properties can lose half or more of their value. After the real estate crash in Texas in 1986, properties were dismantled and the parts sold for scrap. No lender got anything back. Nor were the promoters' guarantees of principal good. All the subprime lenders went under along with the borrowers.

A speculator can do well with individual trust deeds if he researches all the factors and lets go of the deals that collapse. Investors and savers will be miserable here.

Hedge funds

Hedge funds are managed limited partnerships that use a variety of investments and speculations to attempt to create high returns regardless of market conditions. Hedge funds are marketed as alternative investment products. They are particularly popular when the major investment classes are performing erratically. But that does not make them investments. In fact, they are pure speculations. Using leverage, shorts, options, hedging, arbitrage, and other techniques, values can double in a few months or collapse.

Consider this: Hedge fund managers can become extremely rich pursuing strategies that will cost you all your capital. Hedge fund fee schedules are entirely different than mutual fund fee schedules. Hedge funds are paid directly from profits as well as based on a percentage of asset under management. Hedge fund managers take up to a quarter of the profits they make from your money, but do not absorb any of the losses. Both up years and down years erode your capital. The longer you stay with the fund, the poorer you can become.

So why would anyone invest in a hedge fund? Your ego is your worst enemy here. Hedge funds can only be sold to accredited individuals; this means only those with large incomes or large portfolios. In addition, most funds have minimums of $100,000 or more. However, if your income or net worth has inflated your ego, you are prone to believe that you will be able to pick good hedge funds or your advisors will pick good hedge funds for you. This overconfidence will hurt you. Studies by Tremont Advisors and Credit Suisse First Boston show that, after subtracting fees, the average hedge fund far underperforms any applicable market averages or benchmarks.

Hedge funds are exclusive. The number and type of investors is limited; high minimums keep out the riff-raff. Investors are often required to sign an agreement to not disclose the manager's secret strategy. Many hedge fund managers are legends in the inner circle of wealthy investors. Get-togethers in exotic locations with fancy people can be fun. Some funds are better known for their lavish parties than their returns. For those who value prestige over investment return, hedge funds do the trick.

Isn't a hedge supposed to prevent losses, not create them?

In recent years, hedge funds have become less exclusive. At the end of the 1990s' bull market, hedge funds were able to pass themselves off as investments. There were an estimated 6,000 hedge funds with $400 billion in assets. As the market cap of hedge funds grew, the ability to exploit market niches disappeared. Results became increasing dismal.

Brokers were able to exploit investors seeking prestige. They broke minimums down to sums as low as $10,000 and sold these pieces as investments, after taking large commissions. Many investors were sucked in at the height of the bull market only to lose most of their capital in a few months.

Only speculators should consider hedge funds for money making potential. Hedge fund results are highly unpredictable short term and long term. Statistical average returns mean nothing because bankrupt funds are always removed from the database.

Fraud is also an issue with hedge funds. Hedge funds are loosely regulated and many operate out of tax havens. An operator can disappear with your money months and years before you suspect anything.

Once in a hedge fund, you are trapped. Before you buy the fund, decide if you are comfortable with the fact that there is no market for your interest should you want out. Your sole source of liquidity is from the fund. Typically, you can only redeem at the end of a quarter. Unfortunately, after a bad period, everyone wants out at once, forcing the manager to liquidate at the bottom, turning a bad investment into a disaster.

Private businesses

Enterprising speculators enjoy owning parts of private businesses.

Many businesses need your capital and your expertise. This is good for the ego, if not the pocketbook. You can be on a board of directors; you hobnob with management. You get to be an angel rescuing sinners. But do not forget that financially, this is a speculation.

Overconfidence and grandiosity are the biggest issues here. There is a reason a business is looking for investors or is for sale: It is in trouble and banks will not loan it money. Your ambition and optimism may blind you to this fact. Some businesses are doing okay but have risky growth plans; they want your money to fund those plans when banks will not. Others are in tough cycles and bad competitive positions. You may believe that you understand all businesses, not just the one you are in. Unfortunately, you do not.

To make money with these speculations, you need to take steps to deflate your ego. Take a job with the business for a year before you invest. This will contain your ego. Instead of being an angel or a director, you will be a low-level employee. Then you will see what is really going on.

For those of you not willing to humble yourselves enough to actually work for the company, do enough research to check your ego. Look at a 10-year or longer track record for the business. Find as many comparables as you can. Enlist experts to evaluate the business. Watch out when you believe that you will be able to turn around a losing business. The previous owner, with more experience than you, working to put food on the table, was not able to turn it around.

Grandiosity can lead you over the edge. Does your ego tell you that this business will succeed because *you* invest in it? This is pure magical thinking: You are powerless over the market for this business and what it sells, but you think you have power over the market.

Hedge against your own grandiosity by limiting your investment. Do not keep loaning money or buying stock, convertible loans, or whatever. Set a limit and stick to it. Do not throw good money after bad. Also, limit your liability. Do not become a partner who can be sued for the debts and liabilities of the company.

If you are looking for fun and can afford losses, start-ups may be your thing. Start-ups are exciting, but four out of five fail in the first five years. You can spend endless hours playing with a start-up. For the right speculator, start-ups provide good entertainment. However, some speculators get hooked on making start-ups succeed.

Small business investing can turn into an obsession and even an addiction. Watch how much time you spend at this. To do well investing in small businesses, you must spend a lot of time, yet the financial rewards are minimal. The odds are you will lose money. Ask yourself, what am I doing this for if this is not about making money? If you work long hours at your job and long hours on your investments, ask yourself how that benefits you other than financially. For example, does it allow you to avoid an uncomfortable relationship with your spouse and children? Does it keep you from your parents, brothers, sisters, or friends? Do you sense there is some reason you are doing this other than money but you just do not know what that reason is? Do these questions make you sad or angry? If so, be sure to work through the exercises in Step 2. You may discover what is going on.

Venture capital and private equity funds

Venture capital and private equity funds invest in groups of private businesses. Venture capital funds mostly purchase interests in new firms. Private equity funds try to find old firms that can be resurrected. Often though, old and new firms are found in both types of funds. Both types of funds buy private, inside deals, although that does not mean they will be profitable.

The emotional issues are similar to those for hedge funds. The emphasis in private equity is on private, as in "exclusive," and not equity, because there won't be much equity left when the partnership liquidates.

These deals are sold to your ego. You must be accredited. You are offered exclusive deals available only to select clients for a limited time.

The promoter often throws in that he normally offers a piece of the action only to institutions. Because you already have enough money to be accredited, your ego is already telling you that you have a superior intellect and have found a special deal not available to the general public.

Inside knowledge is the big hook. Hedge funds buy securities sold to the general public. Venture capital and private equity funds claim exclusive access to non-public firms. Your general partner will claim to have better contacts and more experience and industry knowledge than everyone else. They all claim this. They must. It is well-known that less than 10 percent of venture capital deals have huge returns and more than 90 percent are losers. Yet all funds claim to have access to the winners.

If you enjoy the high of being in on inside deals, venture capital and private equity will be fine for you.

These funds also deal in complex businesses and markets. Those who enjoy business concepts can have fun here. However, if you are a speculator scheming for a profit, you may want to speculate elsewhere.

Accounting issues are murky. The records you are shown before you purchase are based on deals that worked out and were liquidated. In many scams, the records of bad deals are not available. The bull run from 1990–1999 makes particularly good reading, but be wary of extrapolating. Promoters often do well with small amounts of money. When they grow, they have to invest in lower quality deals. Also, economic cycles distort results. When oil is hot, oil deals look great. When tech is hot, tech deals look great.

Once you invest, it is hard to know how you are doing. Assets are valued at cost years after purchase or at vague appraisal numbers. Magical thinking often takes over. You may imagine values and returns based on your hopes and fears.

The promoters set up speculators who do not do their homework. You need to look closely at how profits and losses are divided between you and the promoters. Promoters are paid a percentage of profits and a percentage of the fund value. By borrowing large sums, the promoter doubles or triples the size of the fund and increases his fees while increasing your risks.

Often, deals are also structured asset by asset. If one business goes public at a profit, the promoter gets a cut. If another deal collapses, you lose all your investment, but the promoter does not reimburse the fund. In a typical deal, two of 10 companies may turn a profit and eight go bankrupt. You will lose 80 percent of your investment on the bankruptcies and hope to double your remaining 20 percent for a final loss of only 60 percent. The promoter is unaffected by the bankruptcies but takes a third or more of the gain on the winners.

Some funds can also stir up anger and resentment toward your fellow investors. Funds have different classes of investors. Early stage investors pay less for shares than later stage investors. Some early stage investors cash out with your investment. As they paid less for shares, they also can make a profit at a lower IPO price. If early stage investors paid $1 a share and you paid $10, then an IPO at $5 is great for them and a loss for you.

Private equity and venture capital can irritate you for a period of years. Private equity deals often include an obligation to make future contributions. These contributions are supposedly needed to bail out failing companies. They may or may not do that, but they certainly keep the fund management afloat. These are legally binding obligations. Even if your initial contribution turns into a complete loss, you need to add more money. The only way to get out of this is to sell or give your interest to another speculator. However, even this may not be possible. In most deals, you must get permission from the general partner to transfer your interest. They do not want you selling to someone who cannot afford to make the additional payments.

Even with permission to sell, you may not be able to find a buyer. There is no ready market for private equity and venture capital interests. Often there are no buyers or only buyers at a huge discount to estimated value. This is built-in unmanageability for many investors. They feel trapped in their mistakes for decades. For others, it acts as a discipline to buy and hold, though this can be quite frustrating too if returns are bad.

Venture capital can create herd psychosis. In the late stages of the tech bubble, unlisted bubble companies were able to auction their shares to the highest bidder. Veteran venture capital investors were mesmerized by the huge sums of money they had under their control. Grandiosity led them to pour billions into deals that had no chance of success. A large segment of society caught the frenzy. Businesses that supplied goods and services for the bubble companies accepted unlisted stock as compensation. Greed turned savers into rank speculators.

To take advantage of public interest, many brokers and mutual funds made venture capital and private equity less exclusive. Investments as small as $1,000 are now available. Most speculators will want to take a pass on these deals.

Commodities

Commodity trading is for pure speculators. Commodities include gold, silver, and other metals; crops and livestock; and currencies. Stock and bond index futures (discussed previously) are traded on the commodity exchanges.

You can either buy or sell a commodity futures contract. If you buy a contract, then you are buying a specific quantity and quality of the commodity, to be delivered at a specific time and price. Buying is betting the price will rise so that at the time of delivery you can cash in at a profit. If you sell, you are selling a specific quantity and quality, to be delivered at a specific time and price. Selling is betting the price will decline so that on delivery you can take a profit.

If you are looking for action, this is where you will find it. Commodity prices are volatile. Prices can move from a 10-year high to a 10-year low in months. In fact, these things move so fast that you are not allowed to trade them out of a stock brokerage account. You must open a separate account. But a separate account allows you to borrow large sums, sometimes more than 90 percent of the value of the contract. Unfortunately, contracts are repriced every day, and with high volatility, margin calls are frequent. You have to be ready at any moment to add large sums to your account. On the other hand, profits can be immense and quick. With 10 percent down, a move of 10 percent will double your money. Of course, a decline of 10 percent will wipe you out.

You must enjoy the action, because few commodity players make any money. Commodity prices are not predictable. High fees and commissions combined with built-in turnover erode profits even if your trades are successful. Many players enjoy the unpredictability and the ideas:

◆ Crops and livestock require reading weather patterns, estimating acreage, forecasting exports and imports, and anticipating the outcome of crop and livestock support legislation.

◆ Gold has long fascinated many people. Believed by some to be the only true currency, gold futures are often bought and sold as a hedge against economic and political catastrophe. In the 1970s, the masses bought gold futures and gold bars expecting huge returns. Those who did not get out in 1980 took tremendous losses. In recent years, some investors use gold to hedge against the high P/E of the stock market. Unfortunately, in the last two decades gold has ceased to function reliably in any circumstances.

◆ Currencies take you into foreign trade, international politics and economics, and other exotics.

The dark side of commodity trading is addiction. A good streak can lead to overconfidence and grandiosity. For most players, though, a bad streak returns them to sanity. However, a small percentage of commodity players must get their money back. After margin calls have exhausted all their cash, they use credit cards and second mortgages to keep playing. Some keep on at the loss of family, friends, and career.

When stock market returns sour, commodity trading is often touted as an alternative asset class. While it is an alternative asset class, it is not an alternative for investors, only speculators. The quick gains and losses and the large leverage will cause investors to have resentments, regrets, free-floating fear, and anxiety.

Brokers often try to sell investors commodity trading funds run by professional traders. Unfortunately, a fund run by professional speculators speculating in commodities is still a speculation and not an investment. The sales commissions alone should alert investors that they are outside their comfort zone.

Collectibles

Many investors enjoy collecting. Most do it as a hobby, with profit only a secondary motive. As a hobby, there are many benefits. The joy of owning beautiful objects and historical pieces cannot be measured in dollars. You can also gain admission into an exclusive club. In each area of collection, there is a tight-knit group of dealers, critics, museum curators, and wealthy collectors who enjoy each other's company and get to feel good about their knowledge and taste. However, collecting for a profit is another matter.

You are powerless over the price of collectibles. You can double your money or lose half in a year. Decades go by with no appreciation at all. Long-term returns from even the highest quality assets are mediocre. According to an index constructed by business professor Mark Moses, between 1875 and 1999, Impressionist paintings returned 6 percent a year. Lower quality assets have negative returns.

Collecting herds come and go. In the 1970s and early 1980s, collectibles of all types were touted as sure winners against ever-rising inflation. Art, vintage cars, coins, stamps, antiques, jewelry, and anything made out of gold or silver were hot. Similar to the shares of recent bubble companies, collectibles became barter and could be traded for consumable goods and services. In the late 1980s, most collectibles collapsed in price but fine art entered a bubble period. Then came the crash. In 1989, many paintings sold for twice what they would fetch in 2002.

You are powerless over all aspects of the market. Some items purchased at retail from a dealer can only be resold at wholesale to another dealer. Better prices can usually be obtained from other collectors. Unfortunately, even other collector's tastes are unpredictable.

The big money is made when the wealthy public enters the area. But fads quickly come and go. New collectibles are being produced all the time, all over the world.

Unmanageability is rampant with collectibles. It is difficult for professional collectors to make profits. Transaction costs are high. For a round-trip purchase and sale, commissions, sales taxes, and other costs will exceed 25 percent. Just to break even you need to sell at a gain of at least 25 percent. The dealers and auction houses make the real money, not the collectors.

Unmanageability goes deeper than poor profit margins. These are unregulated markets. Fakes are everywhere. Experts are fooled from time to time, and even experts are not always expert. Anyone can call himself or herself an appraiser. There are 50,000 appraisers in the country but only 5,000 have credentials from the four most respected groups that offer credentials to appraisers.

Resentments and regrets abound with collectors. Some appraisers have motives. They work for the seller of the piece you are considering and they are looking for a commission on the sale. An interior decorator, offering herself as an expert willing to get great pieces for you, should be suspect. She is likely to collect a fee for furnishing your house with "select" pieces.

Currently, few collectibles are hot, but many speculators are playing the field. *Antiques Roadshow* and the opening of Internet auction houses have revived the belief that collectibles will produce enormous returns with little effort. Internet auctions are supposed to have lower transaction costs than traditional auctions. Someday, this may be true, but it is still evolving. Finding bargains on the Internet is difficult. The quality of items can only be judged by photos. Fraud is rampant. Phony items and phony authentications are common. According to expert Harry Rinker, at least 70 percent of sports autographs are phony. Sellers bid on their own items to drive up the price. Sellers post fake ratings of their prior sales, and then sell multiples of one item, delivering none. You must protect yourself with escrows and insurance. However, the costs reduce profits.

Impulse buying is an issue here. The Internet has turned impulse buying into an epidemic. But it happens elsewhere. You will find yourself on vacation in an art gallery and suddenly the sales pitch about purchasing a painting as an investment makes sense.

Serious collectors know a bargain because they have made impulse buys and learned costly lessons. They study the historical price patterns of the same or similar items, calculate transaction costs, protect themselves with escrows and insurance, and make few purchases.

Speculators who get taken either by a dealer or on the Net often consider it an indictment of their own tastes. They rarely seek restitution. Commonly, they rationalize that they should have known better.

This low self-esteem game is not necessary. Dealers and online auction houses live by their reputations. Let go of your self-criticism and demand your money back. Most dealers will refund your money. You should consider suing the online auction house. Thousands of class action suits are currently pending; you only need to join existing suits. The online auction houses will settle with you to keep their billions rolling in on fees and commissions.

Junk real estate

Real estate is a large investment class. Some types of real estate are likely to produce excellent returns short term and long term. Other types of real estate are only for speculators.

Vacation Homes

A second home is a symbol of success and a place to relax away from the stress of city and office. It is not, however, an investment.

The vacation home market is spectacularly unpredictable. Both supply and demand fluctuate wildly. Booms increase both supply and demand. Recessions reduce demand but once built, supply never dwindles. Long-term studies show returns of 2 percent to 3 percent a year, below the rate of inflation.

Overconfidence and grandiosity are the biggest issues here. Everyone knows someone who bought a little vacation home at the coast for $100,000 and today it is worth $1,000,000. In fact, this couple tells you about it all the time. You also know 20 people who bought vacation homes for $100,000, and today those homes are still worth $100,000. However, those 20 people have never mentioned that part of the story; especially when they are trying to sell the property to you. It is important when you look at your vacation home that you remember the 20 and not the one. Your Realtor does not tell about the 20 either. Overconfidence will tell you that you will be the one who buys the spectacular performer.

Grandiosity can then step in. Grandiosity is acting on the idea that if a $100,000 home is going to do as well as the Realtor suggests, a $250,000 home will do even better. And what a great place to take friends, family, colleagues, business associates, and clients. They will then know who you really are.

Resentments and regrets are the norm with vacation homes. Once the excitement wears off, the monthly mortgage, utilities, repairs, caretaking, and security get to you. The Realtor suggests renting to tenants. That leads to tax complications, damages, and disappointing rents.

A vacation home is an expense and not an investment. As an expense, you can judge its value. Is the pleasure of ownership and use worth the cost? Considered an investment, a second home becomes a jail.

Real Estate Limited Partnerships (RELPs)

In the 1970s, real estate was the investment class of choice. Returns were far higher than stock and bond returns and more predictable than gold. People who took the time to invest in individual properties made spectacular returns. However, the vast majority of individual investors wanted high real estate returns with no effort. To take advantage of this demand, the real estate limited partnership (RELP) was formed. RELPs allowed huge properties and portfolios managed by real estate professionals to be sold in small pieces to individual investors. Tax legislation allowed limited partners to deduct paper losses against their income while receiving rental income tax free. Thinking they had found the perfect high-return, no-work, no-tax investment, individuals poured billions into RELPs.

What happened was extraordinary. RELP returns were piddling in the mid-1980s. Investors were told that they had paid too much attention to tax deductions; they needed to focus on deals that made economic sense. Promoters produced charts showing rising rents and property values and sold new RELPs. Then prices plummeted. By the early 1990s, most partnerships were bankrupt. Underneath the tax deductions and the economic sense, the real cause of all the losses was discovered. The general partners and promoters extracted huge fees from RELPs in their pursuit of high-leverage strategies. All profits and most of the investors' capital contributions were plundered. While the promoters became multimillionaires, the investors took incredible losses. Promoter greed can turn a solid investment into a sure loser.

Today, RELPs remain tainted as speculations. Limited partners have no control over general partners' actions and compensation. Tax benefits were eliminated.

As real estate again takes on importance as an investment of choice, RELPs are sure to reappear. Promoters will see another opportunity to legally steal millions. Overconfident speculators are sure to believe it will not happen again, or at least, it will not happen to them.

Farms

The most common farm scenario is this: Your grandparent or parents grew up on a farm. You live in the city and enjoy it. You have inherited the farm, either alone or jointly with your brothers and sisters. The farm has not produced a profit in years. The rent for the farmhouse just covers the expenses. The lease on the land is tied to profits from the crops or trees. Most years, there are no profits. Measuring your return against what you could have gotten in stocks, bonds, or commercial real estate would show how poorly you have done. But you do not measure your return against any benchmark. This is all fine as long as you remain in denial. As long as sentimental attachment works for you, stay with it. Once it breaks down, you will realize that investing in farms, livestock, and crops is rank speculation.

Farmland, ranch land, livestock, and live crops have not kept pace with inflation since the Industrial Revolution. Periods of shortage and high prices are quickly followed by excess and prices below cost. With a few exceptions, only government support keeps farms and ranches viable at all. Small, self-sufficient farms — Amish communities, for example — are thriving in a modest way. For most farms and ranches, though, prospects are bleak.

Romance is the attraction here. You want off the pavement and back to the land. Vineyards are popular for the wine addicts stuck in the city. Fattening cattle is popular with beef lovers. Organic lettuce is the crop of choice in the sophisticated restaurant scene. Unfortunately, grapes are dirt cheap in Chili and Argentina, while your grapes spoil if not harvested and crushed immediately here. Cattle herds can double in size so quickly that they sell for less than the cost of feed. And organic lettuce perishes at the hands of insects and traffic jams leading to the fine restaurants.

True speculators avoid farms as the odds are not break even. Romantics can have some fun here. A bottle of wine with your grapes, a steak from your brand, a salad from your lettuce; they cost more, a lot more if you really told the truth, but they taste awfully good.

Currently, farmland is of interest because the returns are not correlated to the returns on U.S. stocks. Watch for overconfidence. Lack of correlation with U.S. stocks is only a good thing if returns are at least as high as inflation.

Many speculators currently believe that farmland, crops, and livestock are about to turn up for a sustained period. They argue that farmland is disappearing at a rate of a million acres a year as the cities and population grow. Demand will increase and supply will dwindle. However, other speculators are selling out. They believe that supply will grow faster than demand as agricultural technology improves and cheap imports flood the market. They also see farm profits being squeezed. On one side, high-tech seeds are becoming more expensive, energy costs are rising, and fertilizers are more expensive. On the other side, processors and consumers pay lower prices and a fluctuating dollar hurts overseas sales.

No one knows for sure how this speculation will work out. That is why it is a speculation. Historically, overconfident speculators have lost on farms.

Land

Undeveloped land is for optimists. The idea is to buy the land, do absolutely nothing, and then cash out at a huge profit.

Overconfidence is an issue. The factors that will increase or decrease the value of your land are not predictable. Raw land has many uses or none. The person who sold it to you knew more about the prospects than you do and he wanted out. The Realtor wanted you in as she collected a nice commission.

Laziness is another issue. Extensive research is required to prevent a huge loss. Land in a flood zone or on a fault line may be worthless. Well-located land that cannot be subdivided into marketable lots has no value. Environmental contamination has ruined millions of acres.

Even if your land has none of these problems, you are powerless over the factors that will increase the value of your dirt. Cities grow in unpredictable directions and fall into recessions, depressions, even ghost towns. Vacation spots are hot and cold. Farm uses are not predictable. Meanwhile, taxes must be paid and assessments can come without warning. In addition, you have to keep the mortgage current, if you were able to find one.

Land is for pure speculators. Investors and savers will not be comfortable here.

Limited partnerships

Anything sold as a limited partnership is a speculation. As a limited partner, you give up the right to control the investment and pay huge fees to those who do control the investment.

Limited partnerships work as fun money. Stage plays and movies are funded through limited partnerships. Returns are unpredictable and far more often negative than positive. Based on figures cited in the June 18, 2001 issue of *Barron's*, more than 80 percent of the time, you lose every penny invested. Nevertheless, you do get to meet the stars, attend at opening night, secure seats for friends and family, and brag about an occasional hit.

Limited partnerships are also used to sell interests in airplanes, ships, train cars, heavy machinery, or any asset that requires a large capital investment. Overconfidence, again, is your enemy. The promoters will show you how valuable the asset is, how it will be leased or sold at a profit to a highly secure and profitable end user, and how reasonable their fees are for the service they are providing. You will have to qualify as an investor and will be told that you are one of a select group of individuals being offered this special deal for a limited time only. Once your ego has calmed down, you must ask: If this is such a great investment, why didn't the users just get a bank loan and buy it themselves? In fact, why didn't the promoters just get a bank loan and buy it themselves?

Remember, anything sold as a limited partnership is a speculation. Solid real estate, sold as limited partnerships, resulted in huge losses a few years back. Investors compatible with real estate were not compatible with RELPs. The packaging of any investment can affect its emotional impact on you.

In the next chapter, we will look at packaging and other aspects of form that affect you even though the substance of the investment may otherwise be within your comfort zone.

CHAPTER 7

HOW TO BUILD AN EMOTIONALLY SAFE PORTFOLIO

*T*he previous chapters gave you an indication of your nature as a saver, investor, and speculator. Every individual has a saver, investor, and speculator side. While many investments are pure savings, investments, or gambles, most have elements of two or all three. Comfort zone investing requires sorting out the investor in you and your investments.

When your personality and your investments are unbalanced, trouble is certain. If you put your savings into an IPO, you are confused either about yourself or the nature of IPOs. Extreme emotions and poor results are bound to follow. Success will lead to delusions of genius, itself a disorienting and sometimes painful high, and continued purchases, followed inevitably by failure and depression. However, if you put your savings in a government bond fund and your speculative money in an oil drilling partnership, you will have neither extreme highs and disorientation or extreme lows and depression.

Knowing which part of you is handing the money to the broker does not solve all emotional problems. Portfolio structure also determines your comfort zone. Portfolio structure affects savers, investors, and speculators; therefore, all readers should study the material in this chapter.

Diversify or diworsify?

In simple terms, your portfolio should reflect your personality as a saver, investor, and speculator. Pure savers will want all their money in savings instruments, pure investors will want it all in investments, and pure speculators will want it all in speculations. Most of you, however, will want to have some money in two or all three types of investments. The only way to determine amounts is to watch how different ratios affect your emotions. For example, retirees are sometimes advised to have five years of living expenses in savings instruments. They can then place the rest of their money in investments and speculations. However, many retirees are unhappy with the low returns from savings instruments. Being more investors than savers, they will cut down to one year or even a few months of savings instruments and put the rest in investments. This will increase both their returns and happiness. Other retirees will not want anything in investments. They will only be comfortable with everything in savings. While they may start retirement with five years of savings, eventually they will have twice their life expectancy in savings.

You have probably seen pie charts and tables showing asset allocations by age. According to these charts, a 30-year-old should have a lot in stocks and little in bonds and a 70-year-old should have a lot in bonds and little in stocks. Stock and bond merchants, of course, prepare all these charts. Certificate of deposit, annuities, real estate, REITs, oil and gas, tax lien certificates, and all the other products that the merchant does not sell are not on the chart. If serenity is one of your investment goals, you need to determine your own asset allocation based on your personality, and not your age or someone else's idea of what products they can foist on you. Many 70-year-olds are quite happy with a portfolio entirely of real estate. A 30-year-old, new to saving and investing, may be much happier with every cent in a house and a CD until he learns to trust stocks or mutual fund managers.

Portfolio concentration, diversification, and asset allocation also affects emotions. A highly concentrated portfolio of three or four investments is emotionally different than an extremely diversified portfolio with many asset classes and many investments in each asset class. For example, a retiree, Ed, owns a portfolio of three buildings and stock in his former employer. Another retiree, Fred, has more than 100 different investments including many CDs, money market funds, stocks, stock mutual funds, bonds, bond funds, REIT funds, and international stocks and mutual funds.

Ed's portfolio would not work for Fred and Fred's would not work for Ed. Ed is entrepreneurial and an extrovert. He likes to buy rundown office buildings, fix them up, improve the quality of the tenants, and interact with tenants, contractors, and the neighbors. He keeps in contact with many people at his former employer and has confidence the company stock has a good future. He would be bored with Fred's portfolio. Sitting on $5,000 to $10,000 in each of 100 investments would leave him with nothing to do and a sense of alienation and isolation. On the other hand, Fred would be scared to death with Ed's portfolio. Just the thought that a building could go into foreclosure or the company stock could fall into a bear market would keep him up at night. Plus, all that running around would keep him from his grandchildren, his golf, and his travels.

Diversification may not reduce volatility

The myth of diversification is that it reduces volatility. Often it does not. For example, from 1995 to 2001, many investors bought five to 10 different stock mutual funds as a form of diversification. These funds usually included small cap, large cap, value, and growth funds. Unfortunately, many mutual funds included tech stocks, which collapsed in 2001. In this case, volatility was not reduced by purchasing multiple funds. During this same period, many investors tried to diversify further by investing in foreign stocks and venture capital. Unfortunately, foreign markets and venture capital were dominated by the same tech bubble and crash.

To reduce volatility in your portfolio, you need to closely monitor the content of each investment and determine if returns from the content are influenced by the same economic and market factors. Generally, the form of the investment is not as important as the content. Mutual funds that all own tech stocks are correlated. Yet, returns on a REIT mutual fund, a stock mutual fund, and Treasury bond mutual fund are not correlated even though they are all mutual funds.

You need to experiment with different levels of diversification to determine what fits your personality. You might prefer concentration in one asset class and diversification in another. For example, you might keep all your savings in one $100,000 FDIC-insured CD, but own 50 individual stocks. Someone else wants $10,000 in 10 different CDs, but has all her investments in the company stock.

Be aware that, even when diversification effectively reduces volatility, it may make you miserable. For Ed it took the fun out of investing. It may also lock-in mediocre returns and high expenses. Multiple mutual funds in multiple asset classes is a common method of reducing volatility. But more than 80 percent of funds do worse than their market, yet fund managers make nearly a half million dollars a year for these pitiful results. Over time, this can gnaw at many people.

Many brokers and new financial planners are eager to sell you options and other derivatives to hedge the volatility in your portfolio. For example, you are worried about declines in stocks. You can short some stocks while betting others go up. This allows you to benefit either way the market moves and dampens the overall volatility of your stocks. Or you could short the entire market using index options. While all this sounds good on paper, most investors who actually take this advice are unhappy.

If shorts or options are outside your comfort zone, you will not be able to focus on how they are offsetting the volatility in your overall portfolio. Instead, you will imagine the worst-case scenario of the short position turning against you for millions of dollars or the option expiring worthless, buying more options, more expirations, and so on until half your money is gone. For most investors, using speculations to reduce volatility creates more fear rather than less fear.

Savers are always advised that they ought to have some money in stocks because stocks occasionally go up when bonds go down. This will reduce the overall volatility of the portfolio. However, even placing a small part of a portfolio in stocks can be too much for a pure saver. A saver with an obsessive fear about stocks is happier with volatility than lack of sleep. In fact, predictability is much more important to many savers than volatility. A 10-year Treasury bond may be volatile but it is a certainty that in 10 years you will get your principal back and that all interest will be paid on time. It is not predictable what stocks or stock mutual funds will do over any time period.

Portfolio size does matter

In addition to asset class diversification, size and time diversification are often suggested as ways to take fear and other troubling emotions out of investing. These do not always work.

A focus on stock prices often confuses people. You may feel that a $2 stock is more comfortable than a $200 stock. Somehow owning 1,000 shares of a $2 stocks is not troubling while 10 shares of a $200 stock is troubling. The $2 stock trades in cents, up 5 cents one day and down 5 cents the next.

The $200 stock trades in dollars, up $2 one day and down $2 the next. In both instances, you own $2,000 of stock. Fear of large numbers can be an emotional trap.

Looking to buy a cheap, stable stock, you buy the $2 stock that trades in cents. A 5-cent trade is more than twice as volatile as a $2 trade on the $200 stocks. Another investor may think the $200 stock the more secure as the distance between $200 and zero is greater than the distance between $2 and zero. However, a flawed $200 stock can get to zero as quickly as a flawed $2 stock. Stock price tells you nothing about the volatility of the stock or the fundamentals of the company.

Large investment amounts often scare people. It is commonly suggested that to invest $100,000 in stocks, you should invest $1,000 at a time. Quick investment moves also scare people. Liquidating $100,000 in stocks in a single move is often too much. Therefore it is suggested to sell off $10,000 at a time. These techniques are called dollar cost averaging.

Dollar cost averaging is the practice of steadily buying or selling a fixed dollar amount of investment over a period of time. Many investors dollar cost average into 401(k)s or IRA stock mutual funds. Every month they have a few hundred dollars deducted from their paycheck and placed into the funds. A mortgage payment is a common system to invest in real estate one month at a time.

There are several problems with dollar cost averaging into investments. This often leads to vagueness. Investors do not know how much money they have invested. The value of the investment fluctuates even though the payment is fixed. Real estate values are never certain until a sale. Mortgage payments are mostly interest, so it is difficult to figure out how much principal has been paid. With automatic withdrawals into 401(k)s and IRAs, investors sometimes forget what exactly they own. Vagueness is accompanied by free-floating fears. Dollar cost averagers worry they have too little to meet their goals and too much in one investment.

Dollar cost averaging also does not alleviate the fear of large sums. Over time, account values grow. In addition, contributions are usually invested in a few stock mutual funds. This leaves the investor with a large sum solely in one asset class: stocks. When the investors check their accounts and discover how much they have in one place, they may panic. If they fail to check their account until after everyone is talking about a stock market crash, they will discover that they have suffered huge losses.

Dollar cost averaging and other schemes designed to alleviate fears of large numbers and quick movements must be carefully structured. Those unable to handle investing large numbers should dollar cost average into multiple asset classes. This often means foregoing tax benefits and investing outside 401(k)s and IRAs. Many asset classes are not available in tax-deferred accounts.

Quick declines can be avoided by investing in steadier asset classes. Most speculations are highly volatile. Stocks are volatile. Real estate is less volatile. Corporate bonds can be as volatile as stocks but Treasury bonds are generally less volatile. Certificates of deposit and money market funds have no volatility.

Overall portfolio volatility can be reduced by investing in asset classes that are not correlated. For example, real estate, stock, and oil and gas returns are not correlated. A portfolio of all three would have less volatility than a portfolio of only one or two. However, you may not be happy with any of these investment classes even though you could set up a low volatility portfolio.

Form can control the emotional substance of an investment

You will have noticed from the preceding chapters that different forms of investing in the same asset class affect the emotional appeal of each asset class. For example, a saver can buy Treasury bonds individually or through a mutual fund. Individual purchases can lead to bouts of fear that you bought the wrong maturity or the wrong amount. A mutual fund eliminates this fear. With a mutual fund, the mutual fund manager worries about the maturity and the weighting of different bonds. Yet mutual funds can lead to resentment at paying high fees and commissions for mediocre results. Buying individual bonds avoids these issues.

Every asset class is sold in multiple forms. Liquid assets are sold individually, in mutual funds, in CEFs, and in various trusts. Many forms of liquid assets are purchased in tax-deferred accounts such as 401(k)s and IRAs. Non-liquid assets are sold individually, in venture capital funds, in trusts, in partnerships, and in limited partnerships.

Pay as much attention to investment form as to asset class in building a compatible portfolio.

Each form of owning stocks has different emotional ramifications. Investing through a mutual fund may be more troubling than investing in individual stocks through a discount broker. If you invest in a mutual fund, you have to worry about two people's comfort zone: yours and the mutual fund manager's. You must determine if you are investing in your comfort zone and if the mutual fund manager is investing within her comfort zone. With the mutual fund manager, you can look at her long-term record. Did she or did she not panic in 1981, 1984, 1987, 1990, 1994, 1998, 2000, and 2001? Was she correct to panic or was it an unhealthy panic? Did she show excessive greed in the 1995-1999 run that lead to dire results afterward? About yourself, if you are new to investing, you can only guess how you will react.

Holding stocks in mutual funds within a 401(k) or IRA shifts the emotional dynamics. You cannot take the money out without paying taxes and a 10-percent tax penalty. You are less likely to panic and blow all your money on a sports car. However, in some situations, such as April 2000 for tech investors, panic was appropriate. Preventing panic with tax penalties is not always a good result. You also still have to worry about your mutual fund manager, even though your fund is in a 401(k) or IRA.

The solution to a troubling investment is often a change of form rather than the asset class. You may want to hold stocks or bonds, but the strictures of a 401(k) or an IRA may bug you. Saving on taxes is not everything for everybody. If you like to sell often and spend the proceeds on clothes, trips, or new gizmos, that is fine, that is who you are. But don't put the money in an IRA to reduce your tax bill. Then you have to pay the 10-percent tax on early withdrawal as well as have the proceeds added to your taxable income incurring further taxes. Tax-deferred accounts are not for all personality types.

As you gain experience, you may also want to change the form of your investments. You may start with stocks in a mutual fund. Once you understand stocks better, you may want to switch to a full-service broker with extensive research reports. A few years later, an online broker and your own research will better suit you. Some investors go the other direction as well. Beginning with their own research and online account, they realize turning their money over to a mutual fund manager will save time and let them concentrate on other things.

Is somebody standing between you and your money?

Many side effects result from hiring someone else to manage your investments. For a fee, mutual fund managers, money managers, brokers, Realtors, and property managers will invest for you. Sometimes relatives or friends invest for you for free. Using someone else to manage your money can lead to alienation from your money and a sense of free-floating fear. Actively participating in your investments may give you a sense of connection. In today's world, though, most people do not have the time to manage their own assets; others have no interest; still others are barred by social or legal restraints.

Sponsored retirement plans and 401(k)s generally bar investors from buying anything but a set list of mutual funds and company stock. The tax deductibility of 401(k)s are particularly troubling. The sanction of law and the tax deductions lead investors to ignore the content of the investment. Most put money blindly into stock mutual funds and company stock to get tax deductions. More than 80 percent of 401(k) participants have never rebalanced their portfolios. Most sit on highly concentrated portfolios of stocks and company stock but have never questioned the implications. They set themselves up for shocks.

In the tax shelter swindle of the 1980s, investors blindly put money in RELPs to reduce taxes. As losses mounted, the question became: Does this make economic sense without the tax deductions? Because tax shelters led to extreme overbuilding, lower rents, and lower property prices, it did not make economic sense. Today we need to ask the same question about 401(k)s.

With stock prices trading at historically high valuations, does it make economic sense to continue to pour in money? Is a new generation being lured into tragedy by tax deductions? If you are pouring money into a 401(k), do you want your retirement lifestyle determined by 401(k) incentives and limitations? Remember, you have a choice to save and invest outside 401(k)s.

Family arrangements can also affect the emotional content of investments. A common case is the homemaker whose husband manages the investments and tells her little about what is going on. She may be in constant fear of financial insecurity regardless of the amount of money they have. The problem may become acute when the husband dies. Monthly family money meetings can go a long way toward easing her trauma.

Often a busy executive will turn her investments over to a money manager. She may unwittingly find herself with great anxiety or drop into a depression. She may tell others that she has no worries about her money; her money manager is handling it. Later she is telling herself she is incompetent at investing or that she does not deserve the money. The cause of her worry may simply be a lack of research before turning her money over. Before turning her children over to childcare, she investigated 20 or more possibilities and found the best match for each child. But her money is now being run by the first money manager she heard about and is all in the only asset class she knows much about: stocks. Thorough research of both managers and markets, and the ability to admit mistakes and make changes will lead to serenity with her investments.

Whom do you trust?

Trusts are increasingly becoming a part of investment portfolios. Trusts used to be only for the wealthy. Today, they are routinely used to fund college educations, to save estate taxes, to preserve assets for children, and to fund medical expenses.

Bank trust departments create many emotional issues. The donor chooses a bank because they believe that a bank is more secure than an individual, brokerage house, or mutual fund complex. The desire for security often destroys common sense. The mandate of bank trust departments is to preserve capital. However, that mandate is not inflation adjusted. A $100,000 trust should retain its value, $100,000, for life. Most bank trusts succeed in preserving values. Unfortunately, against inflation, the losses are huge. $100,000 placed in trust in 1960 and redeemed at $100,000 in 2002 has lost most of its purchasing power.

Beneficiaries may have the right to withdraw money from the bank trust either immediately or at a certain age. Withdrawal rights trigger fear of change: The value has remained constant for 10 years; what will happen to your money if you give it to a mutual fund manager? It also leads to fear of taking responsibility for money. As long as the trust department runs the money, it feels like the trust funds are the bank's money or the deceased's money. Once you take control of the money, then any losses are your fault and any gains change your identity. Large gains can change you from a victim, where you are comfortable, into a hero, which you despise in other people.

Trust fund beneficiaries may also be barred by law from withdrawing or managing the trust assets. These beneficiaries often have a sense of alienation from their trust funds. In cases where trust income is the sole income of the beneficiary, alienation can lead to dysfunction, addiction, and self-loathing. Earning a living gives meaning to many lives. Denial of this opportunity can lead you down the wrong path. Many beneficiaries of trusts struggle with meaning in their lives. Often the solution is for them to earn their living from work to gain a sense of meaning and connection.

You are entitled to a comfort zone

Legal titles affect the emotional content of investments. Title is particularly sensitive in marriage and family relationships. For example, in marriage, a stock account held in joint names as tenants-in-common, one separate name, joint tenant with right of survivorship, community property, revocable trust, or irrevocable trust all have different emotional impacts.

Any dual name title enhances the sense of belonging if the assets are family assets. However, if the assets are separate assets of one spouse, joint names can create mistrust and resentment. The owner spouse may feel the other is trying to set up a large divorce settlement or death benefit.

Separate names may reflect the accurate legal status of property. In some families, this is acceptable. Nevertheless, it too can cause resentments. A full-time homemaker may feel insecure if her husband keeps his legally separate property solely in his name. Not entitled to the assets in a divorce or by inheritance, it may appear to her that excluding her from the title indicates lack of commitment to the marriage.

Revocable trusts can give the impression that the donor is not committed. Irrevocable trusts can lead to regrets and resentments if relationships dissolve or finances deteriorate.

In many situations, retitling assets improves emotional compatibility. For example, Ron inherited a substantial amount solely in one stock. Ron is financially disabled and cannot handle investing for psychological reasons, although an excellent father and fiction editor. His wife, Nancy, is concerned with their retirement and their children's college education. A CPA, she is an active investor with their joint savings. If they put his inheritance in their joint brokerage account, he will feel she has stolen from him his last connection to his now deceased parents. If the inheritance is solely in his name, she is sure he will let it flounder. She is particularly concerned that the single stock will fall apart and crash. One solution is to put the stock account solely in his name, but give her a power of attorney to invest in the account. This way he controls all withdrawals, but she can invest to diversify and make profits. Another solution would be for Ron to create a revocable trust naming Nancy the trustee with power to invest and the children and Nancy as beneficiaries on Ron's death.

Title issues are particularly acute with most family's biggest savings asset: the home. When the couple purchase a house together, title is usually in dual names acceptable to both. However, often one spouse purchases a home before the marriage as sole owner. If the couple then lives in the house together and both contribute to the mortgage and other housing expenses, single title can cause resentments. The nonowner spouse my feel contributions will be lost in a divorce or death. Shifting the title to dual names is not always the solution. The original owner spouse may feel taken advantage of and gift tax issues can arise. A post-nuptial agreement can be written to protect the nonowner spouse's interest, but these agreements have difficult times in court. In a particularly troubling situation, the solution is to sell the single property and purchase a new joint home with joint funds.

Divorce, death, marriage, adoption, and other life-altering events affect the suitability of titles. When a married couple is successful with their investments, they often attempt to keep investments intact after divorce. This is particularly true with illiquid investments such as real estate. However, at a gut level one or both former spouses may realize that jointly titled real estate is outside their comfort zone regardless of the financial success of the property. Despite large commissions and large capital gains taxes, it may be necessary to sell the property and split the proceeds or for one former spouse to buy out the other. Successful investments wrongly titled can make you more miserable than money-losing investments.

Before entering any real estate investment partnership, consult a real estate attorney about title issues. Tenants-in-common deals often lead to resentments. Tenant-in-common interests are separable. Each partner can sell to a nonpartner without the permission or knowledge of the other partners. Joint tenants with right of survivorship deals are also troubling. Joint tenants cannot sell to others, eliminating liquidity. Also, joint tenants are responsible for each other's debt. For example, it is not unusual for brothers and sisters to buy real estate together as joint tenants. If one were to die, the property would pass to the other. However, if one sibling is a spendthrift and goes into bankruptcy, the joint property is entirely subject to the bankruptcy. With a tenants-in-common title, only the bankrupt siblings share would be subject to the bankruptcy.

Liquidity

Titles can inhibit your ability to sell your investments. Other factors also reduce your flexibility. The lack of a ready market for your investment locks you in. Assets that can be sold quickly at a small spread are highly liquid. Assets that can only be sold after a long wait or at a very large spread have low liquidity. Assets that cannot be sold to anyone at any price are not liquid. With each investment you investigate, consider how its liquidity will affect you.

An asset's liquidity affects its emotional content. High liquidity is good for active speculators; a trader locked in by slow buyers or large spreads will be miserable. Options and futures traders are constantly monitoring liquidity to be sure they can sell at a profit.

Other speculations require time to ripen. Venture capital can take a decade to fully bloom. Traders in venture capital are miserable. There may be no market for their interests or only a market at a large discount. Patient speculators will be happy in venture capital but go crazy in options and futures that continuously expire and must be rolled over or hedged.

Investors are sometimes lured by liquidity into becoming speculators. Many investors were fooled into becoming active traders by the ease of online trading in the 1990's bull market.

Many speculations are liquid on the way up and illiquid on the way down. At the end of the 1980s and at the end of the 1990s, junk bonds were easy to buy and sell. Investors and even savers were fooled by the high level of liquidity. Paying interest rates of 12 percent and higher, investors and savers believed they could safely buy junk and sell at a good price if anything went wrong. Unfortunately, when Drexel Burnham and Mike Milken went under at the end of the 1980s, prices collapsed and interest payments stopped. At the end of the 1990s bubble, telecom and tech junk could not be sold at any price.

Lack of liquidity can help keep compulsive buyers and sellers in long-term investments. Unprofitable traders often do better in real estate than stocks. Real estate takes time to buy and to sell and entails huge commissions and closing cost. Quick sales can only be accomplished through large discounts to market value. Traders in real estate use their energy improving properties and tenants, which increase rents and asset values.

Savers need liquidity as well as stability. A saver wants access to her money in an emergency without incurring penalties and spreads. The biggest drawback from insurance products for savers is the huge surrender charges that must be paid to make withdrawals. Though many insurance products also allow loans against cash values, pure savers are not happy with borrowing and paying interest. Loans may cause them to lose more sleep than the crisis that created the need for sudden cash.

Are you indebted to your investments?

Once you have some savings and investments, you will have many opportunities to borrow money to get more savings and investments. In addition to loans against cash values, stockbrokers will offer you margin accounts, banks will offer second mortgages and lines of credit, and credit card companies will fill your mailbox with new card offers and higher limits.

Magical thinking often leads you into debt. Anticipating fancifully high returns from investments, you come to believe that a large loan with high interest callable at any time by the lender is reasonable. Much of the collapse of tech funds was fueled by loans that only made sense if returns of 30 percent a year had continued.

Both borrowers and lenders engage in magical thinking in bubbles. In the real estate bubble of the 1980s, nonrecourse loans were available. Borrowers were allowed to default on the loans and the lender's only recourse was to foreclose on the buildings; the borrower was not personally liable for repayment. Real estate was the sure thing of that era; both borrowers and lenders saw no risks. As a result, many S&Ls foreclosed on worthless real estate and dropped into bankruptcy in the early 1990s.

Borrowing has powerful emotional content. Offers of credit can cause your ego to soar. Many borrowers believe that now that they have credit they are somebody in the eyes of the financial world. Borrowing can trigger greed. Why put 30 percent down on a three-unit apartment when the same money can buy a 20-unit apartment with 5 percent down? Why be a little property owner when you can be big shot landlord?

Letting your ego and your greed run your investments works out emotionally for a few investors. Some investors are only happy with more investments, even though there are liens against them. Other investors are not happy with leverage.

Borrowing often causes investments and speculations to invade savings. For example, assume you have $100,000 in a money market fund as your savings and $100,000 in stocks as your investments. Your stockbroker offers to let you buy another $100,000 of stock with a margin loan. Suddenly you find several bargain stocks and decide to invest the $100,000. In theory, you have now borrowed against your investments. In practice, you have put your savings at risk. If your bargain stocks become better bargains or turn out to be no bargain but bankrupt, you must pay off the $100,000 loan quickly when you get a margin call. You must either preserve the remainder of your investments and deplete your savings or preserve your savings and deplete your investments. The saver side of your personality will be in trauma. Because most savings values are stable, borrowers often use savings as collateral for investments and speculations. Second mortgages on the family home are common. Bank lines of credit secured by CDs and other bank products are widespread. Credit card debt, though unsecured, must ultimately be paid out of savings if investments and speculations fail. Before you borrow against your savings, consider how you would feel if your savings were suddenly stolen. Then consider how you would feel if the thief was you? Savers feel the powerful emotions of having their savings taken away but they do not always realize the cause is their own borrowing.

Borrowing is particularly hard if you are attached to your investments. Large borrowing shortens the margin for error. Smaller swings in value can destroy your equity and lead to loss of the asset. The intensity of emotion is high. You must have positive returns quickly and never drop below your equity value. Time shortens. For example, stock margin accounts are marked to market immediately. Your positions can be sold out from under you to cover your debt. Anger, regret, and disappointment are common with large borrowing.

Borrowing can also lead to long-lasting trauma. Some investment positions cannot be closed out easily or quickly. A mortgage will only be foreclosed if you fail to make payments even if the value of the property has dropped enough to eliminate your equity. However, a long period of paying the mortgage on an underwater property is quite painful. And the shame of returning a property to the lender is daunting. A forced foreclosure can also lead to publicity of your failure.

Even when everything goes well, large leverage has a troubling side. Quick profits in a margin account can lead to overconfidence or even grandiosity. Grandiosity is a nice high for a while but often deteriorates into a sense of isolation and depression. Overconfidence and grandiosity can also sow the seed of their own destruction. Profits can lead to expanded margin and riskier investments and an eventual larger crash, deeper depression, and bankruptcy.

A large mortgage on a vacation home can ruin the fun of the investment. A vacation home with 10 percent down has far different impacts than a vacation home with 50 percent down. Large mortgage payments require a constant search for paying guests and the necessity to rent on holidays and other times when you would rather use the house yourself. A small mortgage lets you relax even when guests are scarce.

The security backing a loan has a large impact on the emotional aspects of the loan. If the loan is secured by the same investment it was taken out to purchase, then a loss will be painful, but will not threaten your household. However, reckless speculators use second mortgages to finance options or future strategies. This creates stress on the household. A disastrous speculation will either require many years to pay off the second mortgage or lead to an eventual loss of the house. Even when the speculation is successful, overconfident speculators often fail to pay off the second mortgage and reinvest in another risky scheme.

A loan from credit cards or a personal line of credit can be equally stressful. If the investment does not work out, you must pay off the loan from salary or other assets. Credit card loans used to purchase tech stocks are common today in bankruptcy court.

Stealth borrowing is troubling as well. You may believe that borrowing by a stock or bond mutual fund manager or hedge fund manager does not affect you. Whereas a personal line of credit would keep you awake at night, a leveraged bond fund allows you to sleep. This is fine if the fund is successful. However, leveraged funds are highly volatile and can quickly go under. You may be in for a month of nightmares.

Enough about them

By now, many of you see how you have been investing outside your comfort zone. Some stock investors now see that they need to get out of stocks and get into bonds, or real estate, or REITs. Others want to try a few speculations or go into a pure savings mode.

However, most of you probably feel you have a better knowledge of what the investment peddlers have been doing to you than about what you have been doing to yourself. Before reading Step 1, you were vaguely aware that they, the stockbrokers, corporate employees, Realtors, mutual fund managers, and the rest of the financial service industry, were more interested in their cut than in increasing your returns. Now you know in some detail what they are doing. Why, then, do you continue to let them do it to you?

Step 2 focuses on your part. The exercises in Step 2 will allow you to see yourself clearly and make choices that better fit who you are as an investor. After working the exercises there, you will move on to Step 3 to find your comfort zone.

STEP 2

Learn Who You Are
as an Investor

S etting aside emotion in investing is neither possible nor advisable. With-out full knowledge of how you react emotionally to investments, you will not be able to find your investment comfort zone. Even when you are making high returns from your investments, you need to know if you are comfortable. Many speculators on a winning streak experience anxiety. If they fail to acknowledge that they are experiencing anxiety, they will not be able to decide if speculation, even when successful, is worth the emotional cost. Many stock investors in the late 1990s had tremendous success that led to feelings of grandiosity. The grandiosity caused them to feel a loss of connection with family, friends, and colleagues. A failure to acknowledge that they felt grandiosity would render them unable to determine if stock investing, even on a winning streak, was within their comfort zone.

Once individuals and societies can provide the necessities of life, the further acquisition of wealth has not increased the happiness of individuals and societies. Numerous studies show that Americans have tripled their real income since 1960, yet fewer Americans report being more happy today than in 1960. Among the wealthiest 1 percent of Americans, more than 35 percent are less happy than the average income earner. The primary source of unhappiness at all income levels is the destruction of families and relationships caused by the pursuit of wealth. Individuals who rank financial success over all other life goals suffer more anxiety, depression, and physical ailments than those who value good friends, family harmony, self-acceptance, and aiding those in need. For many individuals, the pursuit of investment profits has led to great unhappiness.

Investors need full consciousness of their emotions so that they can feel their way through the maze of money and relationships. To find your comfort zone, you must find your emotional compass.

CHAPTER 8

WRITE AN
INVESTMENT INVENTORY

*B*eing convinced that your emotions have affected your serenity in investing, you are now ready to do some work to find your comfort zone.

An investment inventory will show you who you are as an investor. In this chapter, I will first set out the instructions on how to write an investment inventory. This will be followed by some commentary on the process. Then you will read four examples of completed inventories so you can see how it is done, and that it is possible to do. After that, I will explain parts of the process in more detail to help you through any blocks you might have.

The inventory is a scientific process. You will write down your investing history and analyze it for mistakes and accomplishments. Thereafter you will avoid areas where you are prone to mistakes and emphasize areas where you do well.

After you are finished, you will be amazed that you have never scientifically studied your investment process before. All successful businesses study their processes and improve on them. I had been living off my investments for more than 11 years when I wrote my first inventory. Today, I do not see how I went that long without ever putting my investment process on paper. Now I make an inventory at least once a year.

Here is your task, and it is a big one.

Investment inventory

To do this exercise, you will need paper and pen or a word processor.

If it feels safe, find another investor to work the exercises together. We often cannot see ourselves clearly in this area. A partner is very helpful. Do not use a spouse, family member, or dependent who has an economic stake in your investment success. Also avoid a broker, financial planner, insurance salesperson, or anyone connected with any investment product. Another investor, as interested as you in ending the chaos of her investment life, is the best choice. If you cannot find anyone interested, at a later stage you will want to elicit the help of a minister, priest, rabbi, therapist, or other neutral person to hear you out for an hour or so.

1. List all your investments that you can remember, including for each:
   a. Approximate date of purchase and sale, if sold or disposed of.
   b. Approximate cost of purchase and sales price, or current price if still held.
2. For each investment:
   a. List any resentments or regrets you have connected with the investment. Include resentments or regrets toward anyone involved in the transaction such as a broker, salesperson, relative, or friend. Explain in some detail the actions they took that led to your resentments or regrets. For example, you resent that your parents insisted you invest the money they gave you with their broker. Your mother told you the broker was very risk averse and your father said she was a genius. You also resent the broker because now most of the money has been lost in tech stocks and both your parents and the broker insist that you keep the money in tech stocks because they are certain they will come back. You also have a resentment against all tech stocks and anyone who thinks they are still going to be the new-new thing.

b. List any fears or worries you had or currently have in re-gard to the investment. Go into some detail. For example, you may fear that your mutual fund, which has done better than the market, will collapse. Or you may worry that ten-ants will abandon your property even though you know your rents are low. Explain why you have the fear, no mat-ter how absurd, silly, irrational, or crazy your reasons seem to you.

c. List any other uncomfortable thoughts, feelings, or ideas associated with any investment on the list. It does not mat-ter how irrational or crazy the thought might be. Just write it down. For example, though you have no evidence, you may think you got conned by the insurance salesmen who sold you that whole life policy. You have an odd feeling that the 15-percent interest on those second mortgages is just too good to be true. You cannot pin it down, but you think your husband is doing something funny with the taxes on the payments from the oil and gas partnership.

d. Then write down any impact each investment had or con-tinues to have on any relationship. Examine all relation-ships including with a spouse, partner, children, extended family, friends, coworkers, business partners, and invest-ment professionals. For example, you used your father's investment advisor and then fired her, which continues to irritate your father as he thinks she is a genius. You bought a single-family house in 1994 and did well with it, yet your wife is furious that you did not put the money in the hot tech stocks, because she believes you could retire today if you had. Accepting stock options rather than a large cash salary added stress to your family; everyone checks the stock price every day to see if they are going to be rich or you are going to be unemployed.

3. For each situation described above, write down how it af-fected your basic human needs, including the need for finan-cial and material security, the need for self-esteem, the need for social and family relationships, the need for a sexual rela-tionship, and the need to dream or have ambition. For ex-ample, the loss of the vacation home affects your self-esteem because you thought is was a great investment, it affects the

family relationship because they cannot go there for Christmas, and it affects your retirement ambitions because you intended to either retire there or sell at a great profit and use the money to fund retirement expenses.

4. For each situation listed, write down anything you did or any aspect of your character that caused the problem. For example, your overconfidence led you to buy a stock with little research and your wishful thinking kept telling you that if the stock once sold for 60, where you bought, it can get back to 60. Below is a list of common actions and character flaws. If you are not sure what you did or what part of your personality pushed you outside your comfort zone, see if something on this list is applicable.

a. Lack of knowledge about yourself as a saver, investor, or speculator.

b. Fear, such as:
   i.   Unreasonable fear of loss.
   ii. Fear of success.
   iii. Lack of reasonable fear.
   iv. Greed as fear of missing gains before they disappear.
   v.   Fear of looking bad in the eyes of others.

c. People pleasing, or something similar, such as:
   i.   Conforming to the investment patterns of others or of the masses.

d. Underestimating your investment potential thereby relying on strangers, magical thinking, or other unreliable sources for investment advice.

e. Errors of overconfidence, including:
   i.   Overconfidence in your investment abilities.
   ii. Overconfidence in investment professionals.
   iii. Overconfidence in investments with prior large gains.
   iv. Overconfidence in familiar investments or familiar investment advisors.
   v.   Unfounded optimism.
   vi. Rationalizing away negatives concerning your investments.
   vii. Stubbornness or refusal to accept losses.

f. Impatience.

g. Excessive patience.

h. Wishful thinking, including:

    i.   Wishful thinking regarding your emotional reaction to volatility.

    ii.   Wishing that the high return years will continue or will come back.

i. Magical thinking, in whatever form, including:

    i.   Locking into a magical number, usually a price.

j. Grandiosity, in whatever form, including:

    i.   Believing your investment skills were without flaw.

    ii.   Showing off.

    iii. Acting the big shot or trying to be a hero.

k. Lust.

l. Envy.

m. Jealousness.

n. Pride, in whatever form, including:

    i.   Pride as being too proud to admit you do not know what you are doing and need to find expert assistance.

    ii.   Pride as dislike of admitting mistakes.

    iii. Pride as the inability to admit mistakes.

    iv. Pride as rationalizing and justifying bad decisions.

    v.   Upper class pride-the belief that getting involved in the details of money and investing is beneath you.

o. Self-centeredness as looking only at how an investment affects you and not at how it affects those around you.

p. Addiction to trading or other investment processes.

q. Pursuing fun over profit.

r. Pursuing profit over fun.

s. Pursuing tax deductions over profit.

t. Recklessness, including:

    i.   Gambling winnings while holding principal.

    ii.   Gambling principal in an attempt to get even after losing.

  iii. Investing to create excitement or drama.

  iv. Attempting to distract yourself from other problems in your life.

 u. Denial, in whatever form, including:

  i. Numbness.

  ii. Laziness or simple lack of research.

  iii. Vagueness about what you own, what you paid. what it is worth, or other facts.

  iv. Procrastination to avoid feelings of regret or inadequacy.

  v. Procrastination to avoid dealing with changes.

  vi. Blaming others when you are responsible.

  vii. Rationalizing away all bad news, even into bankruptcy.

  viii. Sentimental attachment, such as attachment to the old family farm or the inherited shares of a stock.

 w. Loyalty to an investment, despite poor or horrendous returns.

 x. Gullibility, due to any cause, including:

  i. Trust of highly educated people.

 y. Lack of experience.

 z. Lack of emotional maturity.

aa. Wrong personality type, including

  i. An introvert in an extrovert investment or vice versa.

  ii. A numbers person in an idea investment or vice versa.

bb. Guilt about having money.

cc. Self-destructive attempts to lose money.

dd. Buying, selling, or holding due to the belief that it is patriotic.

ee. Any other character flaw that occurs to you, no matter how unusual or embarrassing.

◆ ◆ ◆

As you can see, this is no small task. However, if you are interested in being free from the trauma of investing, this is the route.

If there is no problem, then there is no solution

The benefits of the inventory are enormous. Decades of mistakes will come to light. Solutions will be obvious.

People are not capable of remembering directly the chain of logic and emotional reaction that led them to the wrong portfolio. All that remains from a bad investment are resentments, fears, uncomfortable thoughts and feelings, and broken relationships.

Bill Wilson lost a fortune when the stock market declined 90 percent between 1929 and 1933. Once a very successful investor, by 1933 he was bankrupt. Finally, through the aid of a friend, he was told he had to get rid of his resentments, fears, uncomfortable feelings, and relationship issues around his lost fortune. To do so, he and several others who had lost all in the Depression, developed the 12 steps that are the basis of all 12-step programs. The investment inventory process is derived from the 12 steps.

Studies show few investors remember how they got in their investment mess. All they remember is residue of the mess—fear, resentment, uncomfortable feelings, and relationship troubles. The genius of the 12 steps is that they jump from the residue of investment incompatibility directly to the cause: personality characteristics. A detailed memory of how the mess came into being is not required to complete an inventory.

Emotionless investing is the opposite of the inventory process. Emotionless investing is neither desirable nor possible. What is often described as emotionless investing is numb investing. Numb investing is as dangerous as numb driving. Numb drivers are a danger to themselves and others. Numb investors are prone to a huge range of mistakes including borrowing large sums and gambling it away on sure losing speculations.

Throughout the investment world, it is stated that fear and greed are the enemy of good investment results. The ideal investor has no fear, greed, or other emotion that could interfere with the pursuit of the highest investment returns. Unfortunately, for those of us who would like to improve our investment results, total lack of emotion is not an option. (The only time a human being has a total lack of emotion is when he or she is dead.)

Emotion is not the enemy of good investing. Emotional incompatibility is the problem. Calm investing is fine. When we feel calm, we do good research and make reasoned decision. However, investments change and we change. Calm comes and goes, but we still need to deal with profits, losses, sales pressures, corporate accounting maneuvers, needy tenants, and all aspects of the investment environment. We also have to deal with money needs thrust on us by forced retirement, a leaky roof, divorce, marriage, illness, downsizing, and all of life's ups and downs. The trick is to know all your emotions and use them to navigate through the changes. For example, you should act on fear when it tells you to get out of an investment that will go down and stay down whereas calm may have led you to stay in too long. You should act on greed if it directs you into strong performing securities. Calm might have kept you out of those securities.

Fear and greed

All aspects of your emotional makeup come into play in investing. Most commentary on emotions and investing look at fear and greed as the main investment emotions. Fear is an important investment emotion. Greed is rare.

Fear comes in 100 forms. Fear of loss is the only fear most commentators discuss. Fear of loss explains some investment mistakes. Fear of loss can lead to panic. But other fears are equally important. Fear of success can lead to investing in speculations that are sure to fail. Fear of people can lead to avoiding financial advisors and investment experts. Fear of failure leads many investors to stay out of investments that are promising where greed would have led them to invest. An emotional inventory that does not include fear in all its forms is incomplete. Yet fear in all its manifestations is only one of many troublesome investment emotions.

Greed is commonly seen as the emotion that leads investors into overpriced bubbles. However, greed is only one of many emotions responsible for buying bubbles. Many who were caught up in the tech bubble had no greed. People pleasing often results in investors purchasing whatever their friends, brokers, or colleagues are buying. Jealousy, envy, lack of experience, overconfidence, wishful thinking, resentment of taxes and therefore, pursuing tax deductions, and many other emotions are common in bubbles.

Greed is not the opposite of fear. Greed, when analyzed, is best seen as a form of fear: fear plus ego. Greed results when fear tells the mind that there is not and never will be enough to go around and ego tells it to get all it can while the getting is good.

More bubble investors suffer from overconfidence than greed. Overconfident investors see abundance, not scarcity. They believe the market is fairly priced and will continue to give high returns as it has in the past.

Greed is an uncommon investment emotion. Most investors never experience greed. IPOs with limited shares and huge demand bring out greed. Greedy investors are willing to make deals and even pay bribes to get in on hot IPOs. Unique parcels of real estate sometimes bring out greed. Believing that there is only one good location, location, location, real estate investors sometimes bid property prices beyond any reasonable level.

Resentment

Resentment is as important as fear. Resentment is a common reaction to investment failure. Resentment is regret or anger played repeatedly in your mind. As the thoughts replay time after time, they are embellished and enlarged. Resentment can spread from resentment of the market to resentment of your broker, money manager, or mutual fund manager to resentment of your husband, wife, or brother-in-law who suggested you invest, to resentment of yourself.

Failing to overcome resentment is toxic. For example, in the early 1990s, a novice investor, pursuing an early retirement, began investing with stock options. Using complex strategies advocated by an options advisor, he quickly tripled his money. Telling himself he had the key to quick riches and early retirement, overconfidence led him to borrow against his house to double his capital. Three months later, he had no money, a large second mortgage, and a resentment. Every time he made a mortgage payment, the resentment grew. At first, he resented stock options, then the advisory service, then his stockbroker who should have advised him against using options, and finally he resented the stock market in all its forms. Sitting in his resentment, he missed the entire 1990's bull market, declining to fund his 401(k), and leaving all his savings in his checking account. He learned from the options debacle something about options: None but exceptional professional investors make money with them. Unfortunately, he learned nothing about himself, about his own resentments. Failing to acknowledge and overcome his resentments, his retirement dream was further away than when he began investing.

Situational differences

The mix of emotions triggered by investing is sometimes complex. Co-dependence plays a big role in the misery many experience around investing, as does mass psychology. Your investments must be compatible with your relationship, family, work, and the investment community. What might work for you in isolation may not work for you in relation to others. Some examples:

- A husband, who enjoys the thrills of technology, cannot buy high-tech stocks because when he does, his wife cannot sleep at night.

- A wife, living separately from her estranged husband, can buy and sell at will without worrying about taxes because the guilty husband, having an affair and living with the mistress, still files a joint return and pays all the taxes.

- Real estate is the family investment of choice. The grandparents owned it, the parents owned it, and now you must own it.

- Once divorce enters the relationship, the stresses of inappropriate investments get magnified. Husband is happy with stocks, wife with money market funds, yet they actually have everything in her employer's company stock and two homes. The legal tangle allocating these inappropriate assets in divorce will breed resentments and hate beyond comprehension.

- Everybody at the office has options and stock in the company; can you sell yours and fit in or even keep your job?

- A tenured professor with a generous pension plan can have a very casual relationship to the markets, whereas a self-employed executive must pay close attention to his Keogh and other investments.

Often, situational differences determine the intensity of emotions in investing.

- Retirees are more dependent on their investment success so the relationship is more intense. A 10 percent decline leads to a vision of living out of a shopping cart on the street. On the other hand, retirement savers see the decline as an opportunity to buy a dip.

- Families with many children to feed, cloth, house, and educate have higher investment stress than singles.

- Singles with no family safety net have higher investment stress than singles from wealthy families.

Personality types

Different personality types need to invest differently to be happy. An extrovert needs constant contact with brokers, tenants, managements, or other investors. An introvert is happiest alone reading reports and planning for contingencies.

A pure numbers person will need to invest differently than a pure idea person. Most people, of course, are comfortable with some mix. For those on either extreme, very different investments are compatible. An idea person, such as a painter, in a numbers investment has a great deal of fear. Options, derivatives, value stocks, bonds, and fixed income investments are very numbers driven. Idea stocks, often growth stocks, are more comfortable for idea people. On a standard risk test, growth stocks have greater volatility but idea people are more comfortable with them because they get the concepts. High P/Es don't bother them. In fact, they do not react to them. A pure idea investor is not concerned about the numbers, whether they are positive or negative. Brokers will try to sell bonds to an idea person with little savings, not realizing she would be a ready buyer of growth stocks. The growth story and other concepts appeal to her. The story works out, she is happy. The story does not work out, she will be disappointed but have enjoyed following the tale. Bonds, even if they outperform growth stocks, will feel like a drag to her.

By now, you probably have some ideas about what you will write in your inventory. Let's take a look at four completed inventories to stimulate you to begin.

4 stories

Here are four inventories, derived from excerpts of actual investors' inventories. Names and details have been changed to protect confidentiality. In addition, the prose and format have been rewritten to improve readability. Your own inventory, like my inventories, is fine in outline form and in phases and spotty grammar. The only person who needs to be able to read your inventory is you.

As you read these inventories, look for similarities to your own story. No story will be exactly like yours, but each may remind you of something you did or something you thought about doing. After you have read these inventories, it will be time for you to write your own.

◆ Kathleen ◆

Before I was married and had my two daughters, I really had no investments. I have a doll collection, still at my mother's house, which I started when I was 6 years old. In college, I started a savings account for emergencies and I still have it. A few years later, I bought an IRA but then I cashed it in so I could spend a month in Europe. I don't regret that. A little while later, I met my husband.

Company stock

My big regrets are concerning the 401(k). I have been contributing every month for 12 years. Half my money goes into a GIC and the other half goes into the company stock. Then the company matches my contribution with company stock. This is a real resentment because I play this over and over again in my head. In early 2000, I had more than $600,000. Now I have less than $180,000. I am angry at everybody I work with that thought it was a good idea to keep buying the stock. I am angry at the company for matching my contributions with stock instead of something good. I mean, stock is just paper. It doesn't cost them anything. I am angry at myself for not selling when I had a chance.

What does it affect? It affects my financial security and my relationship with my daughters. The plan was for me to quit work for five years when I got to $750,000 and be a stay-at-home mom. I have never done that. Even when I took the maternity leaves, I was working on projects that couldn't go on without me. The plan was for my husband to keep working and I would be a homemaker and live off investments, too. Now I don't see how I will ever get to stay home.

My character defect was that I was just daydreaming about quitting. There was something like greed, but not that strong; $600,000 was plenty. I didn't need to wait for it to get to $750,000. I was locked on to a magic number. The main thing was simply ignoring the stock. I did not ever look at an analyst report about the company or do any research of any kind. Overconfidence was part of it. I never talked to a broker about it, nothing. And, as far as I know, no one in the company ever looked at the P/E or any of those things you are supposed to consider. It was just this gift, like winning a small lotto, and then it was gone. It wasn't greed. It was complacency. The other character defect is this: I thought that if you just put your money in the 401(k) and the company put in company stocks, then there was nothing else to do. I was lured by the tax deductions. But more than that, the magical thinking that a 401(k) was self-sustaining was my downfall. Somehow, I just thought the company was taking care of my retirement and I just had to focus on my work.

Continuing to add to the 401(k)

I also have fears about the contributions I continue to make. Half my contribution still goes to stock and the company still matches my contribution with stocks. Now my fears are that every contribution is a waste. A few years from now, I will look back and think what a fool I was to throw all that money down the toilet. In the last month, I read several articles about the company. Some still say the stock is overpriced and others think it has hit bottom. For a while I was thinking, the price dropped so low, how much lower can it go, it must be a bargain. Well, one of our competitors went bankrupt. If they could go out of business, we could go out of business.

This affects my self-esteem. I feel like a fool contributing to the 401(k). This affects my husband. I take the maximum contributions because he doesn't have a retirement plan other than the IRAs we invest in some years. Now he is confused about this thing. It affects our financial security. We may have nothing when we retire.

My part is people pleasing for sure. I am still in the company stock because I am a loyal little employee and don't want to upset anybody by taking my money out. I was in denial and wishful thinking that the stock price couldn't go much lower, but I don't think that anymore. It also may be that I am just a saver and not an investor and certainly I am not a speculator. I am just so angry about this thing and worried all the time about the stock.

Guaranteed Investment Contract

The other investment is my contribution that goes into the GIC.

I am a little resentful of that because now I realize I have not made much money on the GIC when I could have made so much more in any of the stock funds in the 401(k). Although that might not be true anymore. On the other hand, at least it didn't crash. In fact, I don't have any fears that the GIC will ever lose value or not pay interest.

My part is that I was complacent. I never really looked into the other funds and the other possibilities. I just wanted something that was guaranteed for half of the money. This is not really a problem. I have not worried about this part of the money. But I should look and see if there is something better. On the other hand, maybe I am a saver and not an investor. I would rather have a small resentment about low returns and no fear than a big resentment and huge fear from the company stock. Either way I keep working, so why not go with the no fear savings and then I am at least happy when I am home and not on the phone talking to my friends about where the stocks are going next. Before my husband, I used to date a guy who took me to Paris, Rome, and Bali. He also slept with a friend of mine, told me an incredible series of lies, and tried to sleep with my sister. Stocks are like that for me. No long-term potential. I need something more reliable.

◆ Todd ◆

My biggest investment during my first marriage was the house. I put all my savings into the down payment and then every month for seven years I paid at least $100 extra on the mortgage. I had no other investments those years. My plan was to get the mortgage paid off and then make other investments.

Home equity

I resent that my ex-wife got the house in the divorce. I got nothing, but I didn't have to pay any support. I resent that she has not taken care of the house either. She still lives there, more than 20 years later, and the neighborhood is now run-down and the house is falling apart, hasn't ever been painted, looks awful. The uncomfortable feelings are that it makes me sad that she lives that way and embarrassed that I ever lived in a house that is so run- down.

Losing the house in the divorce affected my self-esteem, my financial security, and my ambition to own a house free and clear.

My real mistake was fear about investing, fear that I would lose money in stocks, bonds, tax shelters, or anything else. So instead, I put everything in one place, the house, and then ended up losing it all. The other side to that is that it seemed like such a sure thing, a house. Pride has something to do with it. It was very hard to see how I could have been so wrong. It is magical thinking that there are sure things when there are not. Pride of home ownership led me to believe that once I bought the house it was the only thing that mattered investment wise. I thought I had the perfect investment and would not even consider the alternatives. It is hurt pride that makes me so sad when I see that house and that neighborhood now. It is not just that I lost the house in the divorce, but even if I stayed there, the neighborhood fell apart, and the house would have been a lousy investment. Also, my ex-wife was very committed to buying a house when we were still young and all our friends lived in apartments. There was an element of people pleasing on my part both in buying the house and in giving it to her in the divorce, as that was all she ever wanted.

Real estate limited partnerships

After I got the divorce, I started working more and making much more money. That's when the real investments started. I have a big resentment against real estate limited partnerships (RELPs) and the stockbroker who sold them to me. He showed me some fancy brochures and charts with returns of 20 percent to 30 percent a year and tax shelter savings and so on. For three years, each December, I put $10,000 in a partnership, just in time to get tax deductions for the year. I stopped buying them when they changed the law so you could not get tax deductions anymore. Today, almost 20 years later, I have gotten less than $2,000 back from my $30,000.

Those losses affected my financial security somewhat, but they affected my self-esteem more.

My part was that I thought I knew real estate when all my experience was really just with buying one house. Also, I was optimistic and overconfident based on the fact that real estate tax shelters were hot. I didn't do any research. I only read the brochures, never the prospectuses. I mostly looked at the charts. I told myself I was too busy. Plus it was a status symbol to own a tax shelter. It meant that I made enough money to need to shelter taxes. I felt like a big shot. Resentment against taxes was part of it. Also, people pleasing. It made that broker so happy when I bought those things.

Commercial real estate

Some of my investments have worked out. I own parts of several buildings with two different groups of friends and we have made a lot of money. This includes our office complex and the two buildings next door. Probably because this has all worked out, there are no resentments and few fears. These are well-located buildings with high quality tenants with steady businesses. The only fear is that the local economy drops into a depression. We did fine in the recession of 1991. The only uncomfortable thought is why did I make all the other bad investments that I am going to describe when I had found something that worked for me. Owning these building has some impact on my relationship with the other tenants. They treat me maybe more carefully than they would someone else. That is fine. However, it makes it hard to ever get to know any of them. My part in the good investments was that I did do a lot of research. I took several classes on buying real estate. Read books. Became an expert.

Options

In 1994, I took a loss of $40,000 on an options deal. I have always kept some money in a few stocks but have not paid much attention to the stocks and usually don't return calls from my broker. But in 1994 he had this options trading partnership. The stock market was slow and had been for a while. He said the investment made more than 100 percent in 1993. I distinctly remember saying to him, "That sounds too good to be true." He was very slick. He said something about just set aside your skepticism a minute and investigate it. So I agreed to take a look at it. According to the brochures, it had made more than 100 percent in both 1992 and 1993. It talked about how everything was hedged, so there was little risk of loss but plenty of chance of making big returns. At the same time, a client paid me $50,000 as a retainer on a big project. I sent the whole $50,000 to my broker and put it in the options deal. Every report I got from then on was bleak. Nine months later, I was able to get $10,000 back.

I have resentments against the broker, the options operators, and myself. I also have the uncomfortable feeling that that broker got a big cut of my money. The biggest thing was the impact on my current wife. I didn't tell her about the deal until it was under and then not much until I finally got out of it. She had about 100 things she would have rather done with that $40,000. I closed the brokerage account and gave her the $10,000 in cash so she could remodel the kids' bathroom. But she is still angry about that one.

That affected my financial security, my self-esteem, and my family and sex life.

My part was definitely greed. I got that retainer and needed to do a few months work for it. Then I saw that I could double that money with no work. The greed blew me right past the "too good to be true" skepticism. The greed told me it was too good to be true for ordinary people but not for me. Laziness was part of it, too. I just didn't want to take time out from the office to investigate the thing. I really knew nothing about options. If I had gone to some classes and read some books, I would have seen that the strategies these guys were using would not work when interest rates rose and that is what happened in 1994. Also, I make impulse buys when I have cash sitting around. I am impatient and cannot let cash just sit in a checking account while I figure out what to do with it. If I had been paid in installments, I would never have put such a large sum in one deal like that. Also, people pleasing. I was trying to make that broker's day, and I did.

Tech stocks

At least on this last one, I was not alone. As did everybody else, I lost money in the tech wreck. I kept hearing stories of people making huge sums in tech stocks. Plus, everybody I knew was getting on the Internet and buying computers. The kids each had to have their own computer. Then the guy across the street came home with a new BMW sports car after cashing in some stocks. So in 1998 I opened an online brokerage account, subscribed to a tech newsletter, and every month I added between $1,000 and $10,000 to the account, depending on how much extra cash I had and how optimistic I was. I bought just about everything this newsletter recommended. Most of my stuff doubled the first six months, then at the beginning of 2000 it all doubled again. I kept buying more stuff as prices declined through 2000, but by December 2000, I was paralyzed. I haven't bought or sold anything since. Because I have not been able to add up how much I put in, I am not sure how much I lost. My guess is I put in about $100,000, well maybe $150,000, and I have about $40,000 in the account now.

I certainly have fear that prices will go lower, much lower. I have fear my wife will find out about this one. She knows a little bit, but not much. One reason I keep vague on the details is so if she asks about it I can honestly say I do not know. This definitely affects my relationship with my wife because I don't like keeping secrets from her and I don't like her getting mad at me when I tell her what happened.

My part was certainly lack of research. I didn't do any research other than read the newsletter. Laziness again. Also, there was a big high involved. Clicking on a mouse after I filled out the buy order was always a thrill. The illusion of power over markets and money, particularly a stock that doubled a few weeks later. There was something too about being part of the scene, part of the in-crowd of day traders and Internet people. It was very modern and trendy. Because I'm 52 years old, that thing about feeling young again was definitely a factor. It was probably like having an affair with a younger woman and keeping it secret. Here I had no broker, but there was again a people-pleasing thing. I thought it would make the newsletter writer happy if he knew I was a loyal follower of his recommendations. The biggest cause of the losses, though, was that I could not get the numbers out of my head. I paid 30 for Cisco, I saw it hit 60, so when it dropped to 40 or 20 or 11, I kept thinking, if it was once at 60, it will get there again and then I will sell. I focused entirely on the numbers. Frankly, I have no idea what Cisco or any of these companies really do. I know now I need to research each company and its market and decide if I want to own that business, not that price. Then I can sell the ones I don't want and move on. On the other hand, maybe stocks or anything that can be bought and sold at the click of a mouse or even through a broker does not work for me. Over-confident, impulse buying is a theme here. I do better with real estate deals that take months to put together and then more months to close. Plus, I don't have those prices staring at me from the computer or from the newspaper.

◆ Marcus ◆

I have been investing in different things for more than 50 years and have been retired 20 years. It amazes me that I have never written down the mistakes I made. That may explain why I have made some mistakes more than once. Considering that I have a scientific background, I find it odd that I have never studied my own investment patterns. In addition, I find it interesting that almost none of my mistakes have been due to mathematical errors or lack of work. They have mostly been emotional mistakes.

Condemned houses

The schemes that worked well, I won't go over in detail. In the 1950s and 1960s when the freeways were being built, a partner and I would buy the condemned houses and move them to cheap lots on the edge of town and rent them out. My only regret there is that the supply of houses dried up and lots got more expensive. Eventually we sold off all those houses at great profit.

Cattle fattening

Those same years, with another guy, I had a deal where we rented a cattle ranch and a feed farm and fattened cattle. We made some money the first year but the next two or three were all losses. The price of beef collapsed. We didn't pay any of the costs or the rent the last year and had to get out.

I still have resentments about that deal. Mostly I am resentful at the way the beef market is run. The big guys dictate the price and the little guys get run out of business.

That had an impact on my wife for sure. She was used to getting lots of free steak to feed the family and then we had to cut back for a few years. Also, I was not a nice guy to be around when the end came. I was pretty angry.

What that affected within me mostly was my self-esteem. It was a blow to me that it did not work out. Financially it was not that big a deal. My own business was growing. We had to cut back because I had to pay off the back rents and the feed bill but we still had food on the table and clothes on the children's back.

I'm not sure what my part was. Wishful thinking was one. I kept thinking beef prices would go up. Lack of experience. I got into a business I knew nothing about. It was a very different business than what I was doing.

Oil and gas drilling partnership

In the 1970s, I put a lot of money into drilling partnerships. I had a friend in the business and he always was looking for investors. The first deal, actually, was in 1968. We drove out together to look at the site and he showed me the other well in the county. I put $10,000 into the deal. That was a lot of money in those days. We had a good well and within two years, I had my money back, and within four years, I had tripled my money. That well is still producing a little bit today. Then the next three wells were dry holes. $30,000 down the drain. A lot of money back then.

I am still kind of angry with Tom, even though he passed away many years ago. His kids had a bloody fight over the millions he left them. It took me a while, but a few years after the last dry hole I figured out what Tom had been doing. He put me and a lot of people into an inside hole in the first deal. Then we got hooked and he used our money to play around in new fields and find out if there was any oil there. Once he figured out where the oil was, he used his own money to drill the inside hole.

All that affected my financial security somewhat. It definitely affected my relationship with Tom. But it was a big blow to my self-esteem when I figured out what was going on. He played me for a sucker, and I let myself be played for a sucker. That is the thing that hurts.

My part was laziness. I did not check out those last three wells like I did the first one. There was a big shot thing there too. When the first well hit, I became the big oil baron, in my mind. Bought a new house in a better neighborhood. It was more than overconfidence. I was grandiose. I was certain every well would hit because Tom was my buddy and I was an oil tycoon.

Stocks and bonds with a money manager

In 1978, I sold my business and retired. Several retired friends told me I should let a professional handle my investments and just play golf and travel. That is what my wife wanted, too. I sold the business for 2 million in stock. I gave about a million to a money manager and just sat on the other million myself. It pays a good dividend and they have raised the dividend just about every year. We live more than comfortably on the dividend alone.

The money manager put his million in 20 stocks and some municipal bonds. By 1983, it was down to about $800,000, so I pulled it out and took it myself. I never bought a stock or a bond again or used a money manager. This is one I think about a lot. There are several parts to this. Looking back, if I had left that money right where it was, it would be worth $2 million or even $3 million. The stock we live on is now worth a little more than $2 million and we have been living off it. That is one part. The other is what I did with the $800,000, most of which is gone now.

This sounds crazy to most retired people, but I have big resentments against money managers and mutual funds and any passive investments. When the money manager was in the picture, I just resented that there was nothing for me to do. I built a business; I like business; business is fun to me. I resented that there was no challenge.

Using a money manager affected my ego and self-esteem.

This had a big impact on my wife. For a few years, she had me all to herself and we traveled all over the world and saw the kids often and made a vegetable garden in the backyard and went to movies. Once I took over that money, I started in like I had when I started the first business. I am sure she felt betrayed or abandoned.

The character defect was pride, for sure. Though I chose to set things up this way, it somehow made me feel like a lesser investor than the money manager. Eventually that feeling uncomfortable led to me taking over all the investments so my ego would be satisfied that I had important things to do like managing more money. That is the fundamental belief from childhood that if I do not do the work then I do not deserve to have the profits. That is a character defect. If I was going to continue to spend the money, I was going to have to earn the money. In retirement, it isn't true. Even when you are working you can let someone else do your investing for you. Certainly, in retirement you can let somebody invest for you. But I just couldn't. I truly was too self-centered to see how my taking over the stocks and bonds could affect my wife.

Wife's inheritance

The other thing that happened around then was my wife inherited about $100,000. She gave it to this same money manager and he invested it in municipal bonds. It is all in her name and he is still investing it in municipal bonds.

I definitely resent that she keeps that money in her name with him and does not trust me to invest it.

That again affects my ego or my self-esteem. It has an affect on our relationship as well. It is another area where it seems she does not trust me.

My part there is probably pride again and just basic financial insecurity. I want everything in my name because if something happens, then I want control of the assets. The pride is that I think I would do better with this money than the money manager. However, as I look at these things closer, I am realizing that is probably not true. I think I know how to invest, but I really have not done that well.

Real estate development

In 1983 an architect I knew was looking to build an office building on the outskirts of town near the new freeway exit. I had good success with real estate in the past. We formed a partnership as the general partners and then got limited partners. There was a lot of paperwork involved and lawyers and so on. I put $300,000 into the deal both as a general partner and for limited partnership interests. The architect contributed his fees for drawing the plans and his fees managing the construction. We raised $1.5 million selling limited partnerships as a tax shelter that made good economic sense. We also borrowed $3 million. It took two years to build and by the time it was finished there were five other buildings going up within a block or two and several more at the next exit down. The first few years we were 100-percent occupied, but as all these other buildings came on stream occupancy dropped. By 1990, we were 60-percent occupied, at lower rents than what we got at the opening, and not covering the mortgage. We took on a second mortgage at a very high rate, but in 1992 we had to shut it down. We went through a foreclosure. The banks took it and sat on it empty for several years. Now it is full again.

I resent the whole thing. Every time I drive by and see that building, it sets off some anger. I am angry at my former partner because he didn't know what he was doing and he never put any money in the deal. In fact, he designed two of the buildings that put us out of business. I am angry at the banks, not so much for shutting us down, but for lending money to everyone else to allow all that overbuilding. I am angry at tenants that didn't pay their rent, particularly in the last few years. It was an ugly mess. And I regret that the limited partners lost all their money. That was tough. Many were guys I knew from business or from the country club. They knew I had been a big success in business so they wanted to invest with me. Nobody ever said anything. They got the reports and the reports were honest about how bad things were. But it is always awkward if I see one of them around.

One of the things that surprises me is that I didn't have any fear. I should have had some fear.

This thing had a big impact on my family. My name was on the side of the building. The foreclosure was in the paper. I refused to talk about it with anyone. I was pretty hard to live with for a few years there. I imagine all the limited partners are angry with me. It affected my standing in the community, my reputation as a business man. There was another developer back then who committed suicide after a couple of his buildings went under. That seemed extreme. But I knew what he must have been going through.

Really, the thing didn't affect my financial security. Mostly it affected my self-esteem, my standing in the community, and my family. Also, it affected my ambition. My name is no longer on the building.

My part was overconfidence and grandiosity. I knew nothing about real estate development and yet here I was playing the big shot real estate developer, property manager, investment manager, with my name on the building. Part of my playing the big shot was letting the architect get into the deal with no money when he really did not do that much work. I was paying his way because it made me feel like a big shot. Also, there was a refusal to accept losses. We should not have taken out that second mortgage. I came up with a plan to shutter the upper floors of the building and just rent out the bottom floors and renegotiate the existing mortgage that would have gotten us through till the recovery. Instead, we took the second and just dug a deeper hole. I refused to accept reality. Magical thinking. When everyone else lowered rents, I kept them up because we had a nicer building and a better location. For 50 percent less rent, tenants do not care about that. Also, I was trying to stay busy. I did almost everything myself. Fixed plumbing, wrote leases, you name it. This thing and the next one were a lot about just staying busy rather than making money. Right when I had the building leased up, one of the national tax shelters offered to buy the building at a good profit, but I didn't sell. It wasn't that I wanted more money. It was that I would have nothing to do if I had sold.

Privately held business

For whatever reason, I put $400,000 into the deal I am in now and am now liable on loans for $300,000.

This was a children's clothing company. My daughter had two friends that started this thing and they needed capital. So I met with them and my daughter and then went through their books. I brought in a guy from a big clothing company and he took a look at the deal. He said that they had good success so far but that expanding as they were interested in doing was not as easy as it seemed. They really should have some veteran management. That gave me the idea that I would be the veteran management. At first I made a loan of $100,000 and was on the Board of Directors. Then I loaned another $200,000 and became CEO and brought my daughter in to run the manufacturing. The founders were reduced to designers. We could not compete with the big guys because their factors charged them very low interest rates and we paid very high interest rates. So I converted my loans to equity and put in another $100,000 in equity so we could get better factoring deals and a cheap line of credit. The line of credit got up to $300,000 and was going to be called. That's when I converted it to a note and agreed to be liable on it personally. That's where we are right now.

About this one, I do have fear. The business is still not making a profit, I am getting too old to make it happen, and we are looking at closing down soon, which means if we can't get $300,000 out of the assets, I owe the note. My equity is already gone. I have no illusions about that. I have fear I will take on another loan to try to salvage this deal and lose that money, too.

I also resent the founders, how much money I was paying them for shoddy work, and my daughter, for getting me involved in this deal, and for how much money I was paying her.

This has a big impact on my family. My daughter loses her job if we go under; my wife is angry about that and about the losses. My daughter and her former friends do not talk to each other. It is very unpleasant down there.

This is starting to affect my financial security. Certainly, it affects my self-esteem, as well as my family relations. It also affects my ambitions. I had ambitions to start another successful company.

The part I wanted to play was the big shot, the hero, to save the company, and make a brilliant investment. There was particularly something there about being the big shot for my daughter and her friends. Grandiosity again. Why I thought I knew the children's clothing business, I have no idea. Also, some greed. When I ran the numbers that first time, I projected out 10 years, to the present, and it looked brilliant. The real character defect now is refusing to accept reality. I have to just shut it down and stop the losses, but I don't want my daughter and my wife even madder at me than they already are. Plus, what would I do with my time? This thing kept me more than busy. I needed the excitement and the drama and I needed to be the boss again. That is a character defect. I cannot stand to be just another retired guy sitting on a bench at the airport waiting for his luggage. I have to keep busy. It goes back to that passive investment thing. It drives me crazy.

Certificates of deposit

The one thing that does work is CDs. I keep all the extra money in CDs at five different banks. Whenever a CD expires, I roll it over. Unfortunately, most of that money will have to go to pay the note.

◆ Dillon ◆

My first investments were in 1987. I put $10,000 into IBM and Apple in January. Then I got a margin account and bought three more stocks. One was Sara Lee. In August, I increased the margin and bought more IBM and a few others. Then I got a margin call in September and my wife loaned me $5,000 to cover it. Then I got another margin call and had to sell the Sara Lee. I was out of town during the crash and E. F. Hutton closed my account, sold everything, and left me with about $1,000.

Stocks

I am still pissed at E. F. Hutton. I was going to file a lawsuit against them but then they went under. I also had resentments against stocks and margin accounts. Needless to say, my wife was not happy about her $5,000 and never let me forget it.

It didn't really affect my financial security. I had a good job. It did affect my home life and my ambition.

My part was I got caught up in the bull market mania. Also, I thought I could make money quickly. Lack of patience. And I didn't understand how margin accounts really work.

After that, I vowed to go the straight and narrow route to making money. I started putting money into the 401(k) at work. We got a money market fund. No more stocks and no more margin accounts.

Futures

In 1993, there was an ad about a free futures trading seminar. I was just curious. I actually did lose some money on a few stocks in 1990 and 1991, but nothing much. But this futures thing looked good. I went long corn and short wheat. In a month, I made $5,000 on a $1,000 investment. I showed the money to my wife. She was okay with me using that $5,000. I ran it up to about $25,000. Then she more or less agreed that we should take out a second mortgage and put $75,000 more in so I could invest a total of $100,000. In one day, I got a 12-percent second mortgage with three points for $75,000. At least three different times I had equity of more than $250,000 in that account. Many months I made no trades and just waited until I knew what would work. I decided that when I got to half a million, I would quit. Coffee did me in. It seemed obvious coffee was going higher. Everywhere people were drinking espresso. I went long everything coffee when coffee hit $1.95. I was lucky to get out with nothing. My wife divorced me; we sold the house because neither of us could pay the mortgages.

I don't really have any resentments or any fears about that. My broker put a lot of ideas in my head and most of them were bad and I resent that; he also made a lot on my commissions. Otherwise, it just happened. Well, I vowed never to play futures again and I haven't.

Futures trading affected my marriage and my financial security. But it got me out of the marriage with my wife not wanting any support or any money from me.

My part was really that I just wanted to be a player in the investment world. I was bragging to everyone at work about the whole deal and talking about investing their money for them. People were talking about it. Everyone wanted to know what was going on. People were jealous. I got caught up in the excitement and the drama. Greed maybe, but more recklessness and pursuing fun over profit. Borrowing $75,000. That was about being a player with real money to invest.

Options

After that, I decided two things. I was going to go back to the plan of adding money to the 401(k) and if I ever got married again, she would have to love me for who I am including how I invest. Well, I met my current wife and we kept putting money in our 401(k)s. But in 1998, we thought the tech stocks looked good. We used our credit cards and bought Microsoft and Cisco, $2,000 of each. She took an options seminar. We borrowed $10,000 from her mother and bought calls on JDS Uniphase, Qualcomm, Broadvision, and a few others. We also converted Microsoft and Cisco to calls. By the beginning of 1999, we had more than $100,000. Then we borrowed $10,000 from her dad, maxed out a series of credit cards for $50,000, converted to a margin account, and both quit our jobs and cashed in our 401(k)s to day trade full time. We hit half a million by the summer of 1999 and made a pact that we would get out at $1 million. We lost a bundle in September and October but then took off again. We never played common. We only played calls and puts, but usually we didn't cover anything. In March 2000, we were in excess of $1.2 million. Then we decided to get out at $2 million.

By the summer, we were down to $600,000 and getting margin calls, so we stopped using margin and got another $50,000 worth of credit cards. Also, we had boxed ourselves in so we actually lost money in the summer. We decided to go long everything until we hit $750,000 and then get out. We set it up so a big December rally would bail us out of everything and we could get out. For the last months of 2000 and the first three months of 2001 we kept getting more credit cards and bought everything with them— groceries, gas, the newspaper, everything—so we could stay long as much money as possible. After the March 2001 expirations, we filed bankruptcy in April. We owed rent for three months, owed her mother and her father $10,000 each, and owed more than $200,000 on the credit cards. The IRS says we owe them too, for 1999 taxes, even after the bankruptcy. We never filed any tax returns after we quit our jobs.

Obviously, I regret we didn't go short the last year. We would be rich and none of this would have happened. I resent just about everybody and everything that had anything to do with it: Etrade, her parents, the credit card companies, the IRS. Anyone who loaned us money or gave us a margin account had to be crazy. I resent the IRS. I don't get why we have to pay taxes when we weren't working—taxes are for working stiffs—and how can we owe taxes when we lost everything.

My number one fear is that we will do something like this again. We both have jobs again and a few dollars in the checking account. But that doesn't mean a thing. I have fear we will never be rich, no matter what happens, even if we win the lottery, because we were rich several times and have nothing.

All this has affected just about everything. Her parents aren't talking to us after we dismissed their loans in bankruptcy. My parents aren't talking to me since the first divorce. I have never been more worried about money; my wife and I haven't had sex or even slept in the same bed for months; I have no ambition any more and neither does she. She has a Ph.D., I have a Masters degree, and we live in a bad neighborhood with secondhand furniture and lousy jobs.

My part was beyond magical thinking or recklessness or pursuing fun over profit. We were getting high from this and telling everybody how we were going to buy a yacht and cruise them to Hawaii for a year and all kinds of crazy stuff. There was an addiction thing going on for sure. Also, I cannot explain why we never paid off the credit cards or filed our taxes or never paid her parents back. In that area, and maybe others, we were numb. We were completely absorbed by the market, even more so when it was not working. It was the only thing we talked about or thought about or did. Everybody in the chat rooms knew us and tried to steal ideas from us. What is scary is that I miss it and so does she and we are afraid that if we get back together we will get into something like this again. It's not really a fear, it is a certainty. Right now, we are just in a lull in the mania.

Suggestions about the process

Reading these inventories may have you ready to write your own. If so, do it. However, if you don't feel ready quite yet or you have some questions along the way, here are some hints to help you through.

Though you have been able to read these completed inventories in a few minutes, in practice they take some time to write. Speed is not required, but persistence is important. At some point, you may find yourself trying to talk yourself out of finishing. Take breaks. Put the inventory away for a day or two and then come back to it.

The idea is not to hit yourself over the head with all the mistakes you have made. Accept that you are human and make mistakes, embrace those mistakes as normal human behavior, and then seek to make a little progress. I once put $80,000 into a small company a year before they went bankrupt.

My ego told me I was such a great investor that just by my investing in the company it would turn around. After writing my inventory about that one, I have not tried to rescue a company since, though I have made some less painful emotional mistakes.

The easy way

The easy way into the process is to make the list of investments first, then pick the investment that bugs you the most, and write about it. If you have energy, then take on another one. When your energy is gone, stop for the day.

Then do another one each day, in the morning before work, as if writing a journal. If you have energy, do more than one in a day.

Be aware that this is emotionally draining. You need to pace yourself. The real benefit comes from the end result of doing your whole list and finding the patterns.

Some people also like to write the list first, then write resentments for each item on the list, then write all the fears, then write all the uncomfortable feelings, then write all the affects on relationships. After that, for each investment, they write all the information about how it affected their basic human needs. Finally, for each, they write their part. Any procedure that works for you is fine.

Write a stream of consciousness if you can. Write like a journal. Just let it flow. Keep writing until you feel you are done. There is no wrong way to do it. Go back and add more later. Do not worry about cutting or deleting, facts or statements that seem out of place. Write until you get to what you feel matters and let the other stuff just stay there too. Later, the other stuff may come to have great meaning.

The investment list

After you have finished your initial investment list, search your memory for investments that you may have forgotten. Include high school money you put into concert tickets that you intended to resell, stocks, bonds, and real estate, second homes, whole life insurance, and money automatically deducted from your paycheck that goes into a tax deferred retirement plan. Go down the investment lists in Step 1 to help trigger your memory.

Also include significant non-investments; investments that you studied, or talked about, but did not make and now have resentments or regrets about not investing. Many people have a pattern of not investing in things that go up and investing in things that go down. You want to see if you have any patterns in this area and what the cause is. For example, I have heard several inventories where the investors were offered interests in real estate but always declined because of fear of large numbers. Instead, they invested small sums many times in stock mutual funds and ended up losing large sums in stocks.

Resentments

Write down every resentment you can think of. This is your chance to tell everything they did to you. "They" includes anyone who had anything to do with the investment, directly or indirectly. Write down the details of what they did to you. If your uncle told you that his partner got a tip from his stockbroker, and you used the tip, you may have a resentment against your uncle, his partner whom you have never met, and his stockbroker whose name you do not know. Write down all three resentments. You resent the stockbroker because she should not go around recommending bad stocks. You resent your uncle's partner because he should not be spreading stories about stocks that he has already purchased. He was just trying to pump up the price. You resent your uncle because he has no business giving stock tips, as he knows nothing about the company or stocks.

It is fine if your writing leads to odd resentments. The resentment or regret need not be directly related to the performance of the investment. For example, in 1983 I put $20,000 into a real estate limited partnership. By 1993, the partnership was worthless but the owners had sucked off enough fees to become some of the richest people in the world. I had little resentment about the loss of money because I got decent tax deductions and learned about tax distraction. But my resentment against the owners was a bigger issue that did not go away easily.

Resentments are often directed against people who had nothing to do with your investment. That is fine. Write it down. In 1988, I invested in a fund that outperformed just about every international fund for the next 10 years, at which time I was forced to transfer my interests to my ex-wife as part of a divorce decree. The resentment was against my ex-wife, not the fund. You may be furious that your brother bought Microsoft in 1988, went to India for 10 years, and came home a multimillionaire, when you were investing in zero coupon bonds to finance your kids' college educations. Your resentment is against your brother even though he had nothing to do with your zero coupon bonds.

Regrets are often about what we did not do rather than what we did do. Many investors regret that they did not buy a certain stock before a long run up, even though they researched it and almost bought it. Some investors regret selling a successful investment too soon. Countless people bought Microsoft between 1988 and 2000, but few held on for the whole gain. Many Californians regret selling their first home rather than holding on to it as an investment. Others regret that they did hold on to their first home as an investment.

Whatever your resentments or regrets, no matter how trivial or self-pitying, write them down. These will open the door to discovering your comfort zone.

Fears

Your fears need not be directly related to the performance of your investment. You may fear that people will discover you lost money in tech stocks, not that tech stocks will decline further because you have already sold your tech stocks. Several times a year you may fear that your asset allocation is wrong and you need to sell everything and start over even though your investments have done well.

You will be surprised at the number of fears you have. You will be amazed to find fears from 20 years ago are still with you. It is the extermination of these lingering fears that will let you move forward from here to become a happier and more successful investor.

Uncomfortable thoughts, feelings, and ideas

Write down any and all uncomfortable thoughts, feelings, or ideas associated with any investment on the list. It does not matter how irrational the thought might be. Just write it down.

Impacts on relationships

Write down any impact that an investment had or continues to have on any relationship no matter how petty, trivial, or picky it may seem. Pay close attention here. Realize that what you do investing can affect your marriage, your children, and your employment situation. If you start managing your wife's inheritance, that can trigger her fears that you are going to steal the money from her. If you are playing the market at work and doing well, you can lose your job if your boss is playing the market and doing poorly. Other employees can also become jealous and undermine the company harmony.

Take breaks

Whenever you feel overwhelmed, take breaks. The amount of fears and resentments you have piled up over the years may surprise you. You may not realize you had crazy thoughts about your investments or that they had such impacts on your relationships. Congratulate yourself for getting this all on paper and out of your head. There is more work to do, but take a break and come back to it.

Instincts

Do not skip instincts. It is important to look closely at what instinct is threatened.

We all have basic survival instincts and material instincts. We have need for food, clothing, and shelter. We also have the need for the company of others, social instincts, and for a partner or spouse to pursue sexual relations and reproduction. Ambition is also a basic human instinct.

Sometimes all the instincts are threatened by a particular investment. Fear that your tech investments will crash can affect your material instincts, but also your social instincts, your sexual instincts, and your ambition. The material instincts are affected if you are relying on tech stocks for your retirement. Social instincts are affected if tech investments are a big part of your conversations with friends and coworkers. Sexual instincts are threatened when your partner's fear of a crash is as high as yours and drives a wedge into the relationship. Ambition to be wealthy is crushed if your tech position crashes. When all instincts are threatened, extreme thoughts and actions are common.

Some investments only trigger one instinct. My uncomfortable ideas that Korean stocks will never again produce strong long-term results has little affect on my material instincts, social instincts, or sexual instincts as I have very little money in Korea and don't talk about it with anybody. But it affects my ambition as I have been hoping to make a killing on Korea so I can write an article somewhere about how smart I was to invest there.

Write down each instinct affected. The instinct list will underscore the importance of investment compatibility. When the survival instinct comes into play, investment mistakes can feel life threatening. Denial of the social, sexual, and ambition instincts leads to thoughts that life is not worth living. It is no wonder that investment disaster is sometimes followed by suicide or acts of violence. We all have something in common with those who jump out of buildings after markets crash or who open fire in the brokerage house. Fortunately, you are in the middle of a process that will prevent that and lead to great serenity in your investment life.

Your part

Your part is the most important aspect of the inventory. The prior steps are designed to break down enough denial so you can look at your own character flaws. When you realize that your happiness and possibly your life are on the line, you will write down, with rigorous honesty, what you did to bring about the resentment, fear, uncomfortable feelings and ideas, impacts on the relationship, and what aspect of character led you to do those things.

If you have difficulty figuring out what your character flaws are, look at the list. Ask if in some way any of these character flaws played even a small part in any investment on your list.

No two investors have the identical list of character flaws. Moreover, identical investments can trigger different shortcomings in each investor. If four employees receive a bonus of 100 identical stock options, each employee may have entirely different reactions. One may fear the options will become worthless; another may be overly confident that the options will soar in value and purchase a new car expecting to pay down the loan with option profits; a grandiose employee may offer to buy the options of the others at a premium to their current estimated value; an employee expecting a cash bonus may be disappointed and encounter trouble at home as the spouse expected a cash bonus for a long awaited vacation. No matter what character trait you experience, write it down.

Trendy character flaws

Recently there have been a slew of articles and books proclaiming overconfidence as the major character flaw of investors. However, many investors will not have overconfidence on their list. In fact, the opposite may be the case. A complete lack of confidence may have led you to rely on supposed experts who took you for loads and commissions and put you into terrible investments.

A few years ago, fear and greed were the most talked about character flaws. Yet, you may not suffer from either of these. Do not try to force your part into trendy character flaws. This is your inventory, not a survey. Describe your part in whatever language fits best.

No matter how small a part you played, write it down. No matter how minor a character flaw, write it down. For example, if you are baffled by your tech investments, you might write down, "I bought the investments. I believed they were good long-term investments. I am something of a conformist. I bought them because everybody from the office was buying them. My character flaw is being an occasional conformist, as most of the time I am more of a rebel." If you have resentment at the insurance salesperson who sold you the variable annuity, you might write down, "I needed a lot of money in a tax-deferred account right away. So I bought the product. Maybe I was a little greedy, trying to get a lot of savings too quickly. I was also jealous of Maggie who has all that money in her 401(k)." If you are resentful that your stock options became worthless, you might write down, "I was a victim of sales pressure. They offered me the low salary with substantial options showing me how well other employees had done with their options. Okay, I did take the job. Maybe my character flaw was greed. But I also had those options for five years and could have exercised them early on and made a lot of money. It wasn't just greed. Every time the stock took a dive, I rationalized it away, believing the original sales pitch I was given. I am a very loyal character. But in this situation my loyalty was a character flaw. I stayed loyal to the stock and the company despite all the evidence around me that things were falling apart."

A very small character flaw can have a big impact. Consider everything. For example, an investor who grew up in Texas retired in Florida. While he kept most of his money in CDs all his life, in retirement he put $20,000 into a scheme that was run out of his birth town and whose employees, before they fled the country, had the same accent as he and knew the street he grew up on and the schools he attended as a child. For that reason, he trusted them when he would never have put money in a similar scheme run out of New York or California or Nevada.

Envy, jealousy, and lust

Often we invest in something because someone else has invested in it. Look close and see if this involved envy, jealousy, or lust. Gotta-have-it investors often buy a series of bad investments because other people own them. Every year it is something different. In 1999, they bought tech stocks; in 1998, they bought index funds; in 1997, they bought REIT funds.

Some character flaws are only remotely connected to money. Lust comes up as a character flaw when you invest to impress a potential or actual lover. In Silicon Valley, many venture capital investments were made to provide pickup lines in coffee shops.

Jealousy and envy combined with pride sometimes lead to avoiding investments. Many people were jealous of 25-year-old multimillionaires who made fortunes quickly in the tech bubble. Too proud to follow their lead, some jealous investors avoided all stocks and suffered with paltry returns from CDs. When the tech bubble crashed, their jealousy turned into I-told-you-so gloating. A riddle that made the rounds of Silicon Valley was:

How do you get a dotcom CEO off your porch?

Pay him for the pizza.

Unfortunately, such gloating further solidified jealous investors avoidance of even lucrative value stocks. It also led to demeaning hardworking innocents such as people who deliver pizza.

Patience and impatience

Saving and investing require some patience to produce profits. Speculating is often more appropriate for the impatient. However, both patience and impatience can be character flaws with saving, investing, and speculating. Investors who pride themselves on their great patience can ride losing stocks into bankruptcy. Appropriately patient stock investors sell when the fundamentals start to deteriorate. Impatient real estate investors run up commissions and expenses trading properties before they mature. Patient real estate investors improve the property, upgrade the tenants and wait for the peak of the next up cycle before they sale. Patient options traders often miss the best opportunities to make profits and watch their options expire worthless.

Sometimes other character defects are disguised as patience. Overly optimistic investors are often mistaken for patient. Investors who rationalize away all negatives or who refuse to accept losses appear to be patient.

Unjustified patience combined with blind loyalty is common among those who bought tech stocks in the bubble only to see them become penny stocks in the tech wreck. Many of these investors loved the product or the idea the company represented. They bought the stock, knowing nothing of stock investing. Patience and loyalty caused them to hang on, until the company's bankruptcy, if necessary. Many band together in chat rooms and bolster each other's loyalty during the long decline toward de-listing of the stock.

Obsessed with simplicity

An obsession with simplicity is a common character flaw. Investing is complex. Many investors lost fortunes following the popular advice to buy four stocks and then switch to four others every 12 months.

The notion that stocks are the best investment for the long run for everyone is simplicity to the extreme. Believing this simplicity, many investors blindly put everything in stock index funds, even though they have expertise in collectibles or real estate or other lucrative areas.

Buying only mutual funds from one "family" is simplicity as a character defect. Only buying stocks from a list of recommendations without further research is simplicity as a defect.

Locking in on a magic number is a form of harmful simplicity. Many investors focus on prices rather than fundamentals. If they paid $1.5 million for a building, they may refuse to sell it for $1.2 million even though the fundamentals of the real estate market cannot justify a higher price. Many investors in the tech wreck focused on prices as the complexity of the products and the industry were beyond their understanding. When prices dropped below their costs, investors refused to sell, believing the price would come back to their costs. However, the complex fundamentals of the company and the industry dictated much lower prices.

The do-it-yourself defect

Do-it-yourself investors need to ask why they do it. Some of us have a fundamental belief that we do not deserve to spend profits unless we work for them. If someone else does the work, such as a mutual fund manager, he, and not we, deserves the profits. This is a character defect. It can lead to large losses. Worse, it can lead to isolation and loneliness. Many retirees fall into this trap. They think, if I am going to continue to spend the money in retirement, I am going to have to earn the money in retirement. That means retirement is a full time job investing and not retirement at all.

Doing it all yourself can result in poor returns. Many do-it-yourselfers believe in action rather than analysis. That leads to trading, which leads to high commissions, spreads, expenses, and other losses.

Do-it-yourself can be a character strength. Investors who concentrate on analysis rather than action, work moderate hours, have fun, and feel connected to their investments save money and avoid traps by doing it themselves.

Pride

Pride has often been a problem for me. With many years of investment experience, my pride tells me I do not need to ask for investment advice from others, even in areas that are new to me. For many investors, pride takes the form of lack of humility to accept that you are a beginner and need classes, books, research, fee-based financial planners, and other help to avoid costly mistakes.

Dislike of admitting mistakes and inability to admit mistakes are forms of pride. Admitting mistakes is very painful for some people. Not admitting mistakes can lead to holding on to losers rather than selling and moving on. Some investors even sell winners at the first thought that they could become losers in order to avoid turning a winner into a mistake. This prevents compounding profits. These defects are triggered by stocks and other fast moving investments. Real estate and other slow investments are more compatible with proud investors.

Pride can also lead to rationalizing and justifying bad purchases. While part of you knows you made a mistake, pride tells you there was no mistake: so and so also bought into this hedge fund, returns between 1992 and 1999 were spectacular, the new head of the fund will do a better job than the guy who resigned, and on and on.

Magical thinking

A common character defect is magical thinking. Magical thinking involves a preconception that an investment will turn out a certain way. It is similar to wishful thinking in that we want the facts to fit the preconception. However, with wishful thinking, when the facts negate the preconception, we accept the facts. With magical thinking, when the facts don't fit, we ignore the facts. Ignoring the facts can be very expensive. A common magical belief is that you can make a lot of money with little or no work, research, experience, or investment education. Despite severe losses due to lack of work, many investors continue to invest new money without doing even basic research. Magical thinking is sometimes focused on gurus or successful people. Many investors have followed guru advice without checking the guru's track record. Family members often follow the investment advice of the wealthiest person in the family even though they have no idea if that person has any investment expertise. The rich uncle syndrome has cost many people large sums.

Grandiosity

Grandiosity can take many forms. Wealth by itself can lead to the belief that you are an investment genius even though you did not earn your money from investing. Business tycoons, lottery winners, and heirs to large fortunes often have grandiose notions about their investment abilities. However, a small amount of investment success can also lead to grandiosity. Many journalists who picked a few tech stocks in 1999 became investment geniuses by March 2001. Their grandiosity then caused them to buy their own recommendations.

Showing off

Showing off is a smaller flaw than grandiosity. Many people bought hot tech stocks in 1999 so they could brag about owning them. Many socially responsible mutual funds are purchased to show others that you are politically correct. Similar to all the aspects of character discussed in this book, showing off is fine if you are comfortable with it and comfortable with the consequences. However, you may find a pattern of showing off that creats poor returns and high financial fears.

Vagueness

Vagueness is a source of trouble for many people. Lack of record keeping and failing to check the records they do have, leaves them open to free floating anxiety and fear. Vagueness often shows up in ambiguous statements about investments and investing. "I'm okay, I'm diversified" might mean I have no idea what I own but don't ask me any more questions because it may lead me to discover I have a lot of those tech stocks that crashed. One of the benefits of this inventory process is that it gets you out of vagueness.

Procrastination to avoid feelings of regret or to avoid feelings of inadequacy is a common cause of vagueness. However, procrastinators can sometimes have all the facts set out in nice charts for years. They simply cannot take action for fear that is will bring up uncomfortable feelings.

Blaming others

Blaming others when you are responsible can lead to bad losses. Mutual fund managers are often blamed for losses when you are responsible for buying, selling, and holding the mutual fund based on your research of the fund and the manager. Blaming others protects your ego, but can easily lead to poor investment choices. Many investors set up all their investments so they can blame others if anything goes wrong. Rather than purchase individual Treasury bonds, they will buy a bond fund. Shown good single-family rentals, they will not buy, as there are no property managers to blame if problems occur. Always blaming others, and avoiding investments where they cannot blame others, puts distance between themselves and their holdings. This distancing process makes it difficult to determine what investments are comfortable for them.

Numbness

Consider numbness when you notice something that you should have reacted to and did not. Marcus felt he should have paid back loans and paid taxes, but he had no emotional response that told him to take the proper action. Numbness can lead to an inability to sense the boundaries of your comfort zone.

Self-centeredness

Self-centeredness is a common defect. This is the belief that you invest in isolation, that your investments do not affect other people. The opposite is true. All your investments affect other people. All members of your family, your workplace, and your communities are affected to greater and lesser degrees by all your investments.

Patriotism

After the tragedy of September 11, 2001, many investors felt it was patriotic to buy stocks and unpatriotic to sell stocks. When the market sold off the first week, many of them came to see patriotic buying of stocks as a character flaw. Investors who sold the first week and avoided losses felt both self-esteem for taking care of themselves and guilt for letting others down. We could debate whether or not buying or selling any investment is or is not a patriotic act. The outcome of that debate will not affect your inventory. Your inventory is about how you feel, not about how others feel or how society indicates you ought to feel. For some investors, patriotic buying of stocks is a character flaw. For other investors, it is a character strength.

The more you write about your part, the more you realize it has little to do with money, and a lot to do with who you are and how you react to other individuals and to humanity. At first, you think your part is about investing, but then you realize it is about what other people invest in and how you respond to that. Your part is about what you think other people will say about your investments. Your part is about your self-image, ego, self-esteem, relationship to the world, and to God, if you believe in God. Investment returns matter, not because of financial insecurity, but because of how they affect your relationships with others.

The short cut

If all this seems too difficult, then do not write down anything except your part in the one or two investments that are secrets. These are the deals you are sure no one or only a few people know about and that you intend to go to your grave without telling anyone else. Writing what you did to bring about an event that you now keep secret will uncover a core character flaw.

After you have finished writing your part, you have completed Step 2. You now know how you react to investments. Move on to Step 3 so you can find your comfort zone.

STEP 3

Match Yourself With Compatible Investments

CHAPTER 9

USE YOUR INVENTORY AND KNOWLEDGE TO FIND YOUR COMFORT ZONE

*T*o find your comfort zone, you will study the character defects you discovered in your inventory, sort through the investments discussed in Step 1, and match your personality and appropriate investments. Start by looking for patterns in your part.

Patterns

Arrange your inventory in chronological order. This will enable you to see patterns.

Read the inventory with the person you've chosen to help with this exercise. If you have been working together all along, then sit down and read your parts to each other. If your helper is just now coming to your aid, read her the entire inventory.

After you have read the inventory, look for patterns. Ask your helper if she sees any patterns that are not apparent to you. It is amazing how often the same character flaws sabotage different investments. Just eliminating one pattern can lead to great happiness and high returns.

Here are examples of the patterns found by our four sample investors:

◆ Kathleen's inventory reveals that with all her investments she did little or no research and she was confused about her nature as a saver or an investor. After discussing this with her partner, she realized that she also has little interest in researching the company fundamentals. However, she is curious about what kind of return she has gotten on her investments.

◆ Many of Todd's problems stemmed from grandiosity: He wanted tax shelters for the status of owning them as well as tech stocks for the thrill of being part of the Internet generation. He also bought investments that were trendy at the time and had spectacular rather than average returns: tax shelters, the options program, and tech stocks. He then did little research, calling himself lazy, believing he would get high profits from little work. A focus on prices rather than solid research was common with each of these investments. He also saw that he had a pattern of buying quickly in highly liquid markets and then being paralyzed by losses until markets became illiquid. People pleasing was a common defect in everything he did. He bought the house to please his ex-wife, tax shelters and an options program to please his brokers, and tech stocks to please a newsletter writer he had never met.

◆ Many of Marcus's mistakes stemmed from the belief that he had to do it himself if he was going to deserve the profits from his investments. All his schemes required that he spend many hours working, except when he briefly left some money with a money manager, and then he felt alienated from his money. He avoided consultants and investment experts concerning oil and gas, real estate development, and the children's clothing business, while he put trust in inexperienced friends and family members.

◆ Dillon's part always involved seeking thrills for quick profits and a desire to be somebody as result of investment prowess. Easy access to borrowing exacerbated the problem. He had a pattern of investing borrowed money even more recklessly than his own savings. He also saw a clear pattern of manias followed by lulls and then manias again. He saw that the financial consequences of the manias were progressive. Each

time he started in again after a lull, it quickly got worse than
the last episode.

Patterns can be unique or common

Patterns are usually obvious after an inventory but invisible before. For example, a building contractor had a long history of poor returns in his Keogh and IRAs but could not understand why. He bought individual stocks, index funds, growth funds, foreign and emerging market funds, bond funds, junk bond funds, and many other funds and investments. From March 2000 to September 2001, he saw the value of his portfolio drop from $700,000 to $300,000. Meanwhile, his clients made millions from the buildings he constructed. Though an expert on commercial real estate, he had never invested in a building because of his fear of large numbers. His pattern was to never put more than $10,000 into any one investment.

A common discovery from inventories is that the intensity of pain from losses is higher than the intensity of pleasure from gains. A few investors are paralyzed by losses yet hardly notice gains. Often their comfort zone is in predictable investments such as Treasury bills and bonds. They fail to achieve high returns in unpredictable investments such as stocks because they are out of the market during large up moves in order to avoid the risk of experiencing losses. However, not all investors experience gains and losses this way. Many traders move through losses quickly and get into winners. In fact, they seek volatility to take advantage of losses. Dollar cost averagers often relish losses so they can buy more shares at lower prices.

Some investors have a pattern of falling in love with their investments. Stocks are common love objects. You love the company's product; therefore you buy the stock and hold on regardless of the fundamentals or the price. The love object can be any investment: a vacation home, a rental home that was the first house you ever bought, anything run by the right fund manager or fund family, an idea stock. Occasionally with collectibles, falling in love with an object leads to happiness. With other investments, it often results in a feeling of abandonment and betrayal.

Making resolutions and not following through is a common pattern. "From now on, I will only buy index funds." "Never again will I own real estate." "After this, I am sticking to CDs." Resolutions allow us to be done with grieving the loss. However, they rarely result in lasting change. Everything goes into index funds until something else comes along.

Tax avoidance is a common pattern. Many investors rode tech stocks up and then down again just to avoid taxes on the gains. These same investors put money in 401(k)s and IRAs when better investments are available elsewhere. They bought tax shelters in the 1980s and municipal bonds in the early 1990s. While tax avoidance can improve returns, as an obsession it often leads to trouble.

Your patterns will likely be different from your helper's patterns. Whatever your patterns, changing these ruts results in greatly improved investment satisfaction and higher returns.

Pick compatible investments

After reading the list aloud, with the help of your partner, compare the list of character flaws with the list of investments from Chapters 4, 5, and 6 and with the strategies discussed in Chapter 7. You will now be able to determine which asset classes are likely to trigger your character flaws and which are not.

Be certain to go through the list with your helper. Alone, you are likely to forget some of your character flaws that led you into incompatible investments. Pay particular attention to your patterns. Avoid anything that is likely to get you back into your rut.

Enthusiasm more than intelligence

Successful investing requires enthusiasm more than intelligence. You will learn quickly and do well in investments that excite you.

Use all your personal experience and background to pick asset classes that you can understand and enjoy. For many of you, it is likely that your inventory showed that investing in areas you knew something about triggered the character flaw of overconfidence. Pediatricians invested in HMOs believing they would be better able to pick stocks than the public. When health care legislation ruined HMO prospects, the pediatricians took losses where specialists made profits shorting the stocks. Women with double closets picked women's apparel companies, but were done in because management produced too much inventory.

Experts with humility rather than overconfidence understood that they knew only a little about the investment aspects of their field or hobbies. Becoming specialists over time, they increased commitments and profits, and had a great time. Stamp collectors who studied, went to conventions, dabbled for years before making substantial purchases had a great time and made a fortune.

With the humility gained from taking your inventory and sharing it with another, you can now pursue investing in your field or areas of interest with appropriate caution and good fun.

Balance interest with knowledge of your character flaws and you will be fine. In addition, if you have investment experience that did not trigger your worst character defects, use it. If you have been retired 10 years, investing full time, and know what you enjoy and what you do not, use that knowledge.

Kathleen's comfort zone

Kathleen meticulously went through the savings list with her partner. She liked the idea of CDs. She liked government guarantees and renewing them as they expire. They were simple and required little research. She did not like the idea of money market funds that could be tapped into by checks. Buying Treasury bonds directly from the government appealed to her. She knew she could do enough research to get good prices. She had no worries about market prices, and she was certain that she could hold the bonds to maturity. She had held on to the same investments in her 401(k) for 12 years. Bond funds did not appeal to her. She felt competent enough to do something simple such as buying Treasury bonds herself. She had not been aware that there was any risk in GICs. But she did some research, and discovered that the GICs in her 401(k) were from five different, highly rated companies. She has no worries about making mortgage payments because her husband pays the mortgage, and they plan to live there at least until their daughters are through college.

She skimmed most of the investment chapter. Nothing about stocks appeals to her. Now that she knows how bad volatility feels and how the company issuing stock is not on her side, even though it is her employer, she is sure she cannot trust other stocks, even if professionally managed in a mutual fund. For one thing, she cannot process her emotions fast enough to be in stocks. More important, she does not see how owning stocks will increase her sense of financial security. Knowing herself to be a worrier, she will worry about stocks now as well as in the future. Her feelings about retirement are less secure when she owns stocks than when she owns GICs.

Real estate does not appeal to her. She does not want to spend much time on investing. None of the other investments or speculations appealed to her, except collecting. She does have some interest in adding to her doll collection with the help of her daughters. In fact, looking closely at the prospect of spending more time researching investments other than the dolls made her recognize that she is not an investor or speculator, only a saver.

All this has made Kathleen realize that the sole reason she is working is so she can support her daughters. Her idea of working long hours to produce extra income to support her family with her investments has been a trap. She wants to support her daughters directly by being a stay-at-home mom. She could quit work now, raise them full time for a few years, and then consider part-time work as they approach college age. Eliminating childcare expenses, restaurants, one car, work clothes, and other work expenses, they could get by on her husband's income. 401(k) tax deductions will no longer be a lure because with one income they will pay much lower taxes anyway. She has $180,000 in savings that could be rolled over into an IRA, invested in CDs and Treasury bonds, and then used for emergencies. All her investment worries would be eliminated. If they have any extra money, they will add some dolls to the doll collection.

Todd's comfort zone

Todd was able to find his comfort zone quickly. After working the exercises with a partner, he no longer resents trying to pay down the mortgage on his first house. In fact, to increase his savings, he wants to pay down the mortgage on his current house. However, he does not want any liquid savings such as bond funds that he can tap for impulse buys.

He had great success with real estate, and no success with any investment that was trendy or could be purchased on a whim. He already had a great deal of expertise in real estate and enjoyed thorough research of buildings and the market. In this area, he had never been lazy or expected large profits from little work. REITs would likely be a problem because he could be triggered into trading by the easy liquidity and repeated price quotes. Corporate bonds had no appeal because he had done poorly with passive investments. Tax lien certificates seemed to be a good idea for his retirement years but would be a problem now because he would be unlikely to do all the necessary research. Clearly, staying away from real estate development is a good idea because he has a history of ego inflation leading to disaster. He has done well with existing office buildings with good tenants or potential to improve the tenants. Investing with partners has helped temper his tendency to act impulsively. It also allows him to use his people pleasing in a positive way. In the give-and-take of negotiating with partners and tenants, he can find ways to get what he wants and to give them some of what they want. He realizes that his major concern now is diversifying the real estate portfolio into other markets. Meanwhile, he will liquidate his stocks, tell his wife what happened, give her $20,000, put the other $20,000 toward paying off the mortgage, research other real estate markets, and put together a partnership for another building.

Marcus and the meaning of life

Marcus had success rolling over CDs. For his savings, that was something he wanted to continue. He also had tremendous success holding one stock and collecting dividends. He actively followed the company, read all reports he could get his hands on, and yet was never tempted to trade the stock.

Diworsification was the first issue that struck him and his helper. Not wanting everything in one stock, he proceeded to lose nearly half his money in an attempt to diversify. Now that he was primarily down to one stock again, he realizes that the standard advice to diversify was not within his comfort zone. Still, he studied the list to see if anything seemed more compatible to him than his one stock.

His dividends paid at the same rate as corporate bonds, and higher than CDs, so it made no sense to seek lower total returns in bonds and CDs.

He had not realized he was speculating when he got involved in land and rebuilt homes, cattle fattening, oil and gas drilling, real estate development, and a junk loan and junk small business equity. In fact, other than CDs and a brief period with a money manager, he had done nothing but speculate.

Looking at the lists of investments, nothing appealed to him. Sitting on a group of stocks rather than one was not much different than having a money manager handle the investments. The thought of buying existing buildings made him sad. REITs were too passive and tax lien certificates sounded lonely. Oil and gas were also unappealing. Corporate bonds might be better than rolling over CDs, but not enough better to switch. No form of speculation had any appeal any more. For now, he and his helper agreed he needed to shut down the children's clothing business, put anything he salvaged from it into CDs, and sit on his stock.

He realized that in the past, he had diversified to give himself something to do, not to reduce the risk in his portfolio. The thought that he ought to diversify again was about having something to do. He had no fear about the amount of money he had in one stock. He found himself in a dilemma. He felt powerless to do anything with his investments right now, yet unhappy about the prospect of having nothing to do. He agreed to talk to his minister about this situation. The problem seemed to center more on the meaning of life than on the right investment portfolio. He was never going to run out of money just sitting on the single stock. The problem could not be about money.

Dillon's dilemma

Dillon and his partner agreed quickly that changing investments or strategies was of no use. They were certain that he could get high and then self-destruct with CDs, or emerging market stocks, or junk notes just as he had with stocks, futures, and options. Clearly, he needed a personality adjustment rather than a portfolio adjustment. Also, he needed to get help from Gambler's Anonymous now while he had little savings and no access to credit. When a new mania took over again, he feared it might end up in suicide.

My comfort zone

My own inventories during the last 12 years have resulted in many changes in my portfolio and higher returns. I have learned that I am a pure investor. I do not do well with either savings or speculations. Savings annoy me. I want to put the money to better use. I have a tendency to make impulse purchases with cash and credit. Therefore, I keep little in money market accounts or others short-term investments, and use no margin, no credit cards, even for personal expenses, and keep mortgages to 50 percent or less of property values. Speculations are a trap for my big shotism. I no longer try to rescue small companies with my money and my expertise. Having gotten caught up in the tax shelter speculations 20 years ago both as an investor and as a tax attorney, my inventories kept me entirely out of tech stocks in the 1999-2001 mania. I am compatible with a wide range of investments including value stocks, real estate, REITs, oil and gas, and CEFs. Stocks have become a smaller part of my portfolio. Twelve years ago, I had about 75 percent of my money in stocks and 25 percent in real estate, REITs, and oil and gas. Today my ratio is the opposite. Real estate, REITs, and oil and gas partnerships pay out all income to the owners without the

IRS taking a cut. In these areas, management has less chance to reduce returns to shareholders from the manipulations of corporate accounting and the reduction of dividends as well as the loss of profits to taxes. I own publicly traded stock of modest-sized companies. Many stocks are in beaten-down companies that have lost the ability to manipulate shareholders and must shape up or linger for decades.

Returns are higher in your comfort zone

If you have any doubts that your personality affected the return from incompatible investments, ask if your returns matched those of the market averages. In the past decades, you should have received 12 percent a year from all forms of stocks and from real estate. Venture capital, private equity, individual business, and hedge fund returns are highly erratic, but compatible investors should have received returns of at least 12 percent a year. Oil and gas, Ginnie Maes, and corporate bond returns should be in the range of 6 percent to 8 percent. Treasury bonds, municipal bonds, GICs, annuities, and whole life policies should have paid 5 percent to 6 percent. Money market funds, CDs, and Treasury bills should have returned 3 percent to 4 percent. Gold and other commodities should have averaged around 3 percent. All other speculations should have positive returns between 0 percent and 3 percent a year for compatible investors.

Note if your mind now tells you that you need to be in those 12 percent+ investments, even though they are not in your comfort zone and you have not gotten 12 percent-plus returns when you did invest in them. If so, discuss these thoughts with your helper.

At the suggestion of her partner, Kathleen estimated the returns she had gotten over the years from her GICs and from the company stock. The GICs averaged about 5 percent during 12 years. The stock price was 10 percent lower than it was 12 years ago. She was not sure what the average return was, but it clearly was closer to negative 12 percent a year than positive 12 percent a year. If she had invested solely in GICs and converted the matching stock to GICs, she would have more money. Clearly for Kathleen, investing in her comfort zone would have produced higher returns.

Todd was averaging at least 12 percent a year from his real estate. The income alone from the older properties was higher than 12 percent of his original investment. However, in tech stocks, RELPs, and options, he had negative returns and no fun. He enjoyed real estate. Without question, his returns were higher in compatible investments.

Marcus was certain he had made at least 12 percent a year in his first real estate adventure, buying condemned houses and moving them. He had then lost money in cattle, maybe made some money in oil and gas, then lost consistently in stocks managed by a money manager, real estate development, and buying into a small business. However, holding a large position in one stock had produced returns close to 12 percent a year. He had no doubt that he achieved higher returns when his character defects were not active.

Dillon had never achieved positive returns on any investment. This reinforced his realization that he needed Gambler's Anonymous' help to find a comfort zone.

Diversify with researched investment advice

Consider portfolio structure when you set up your comfort zone. If you are only comfortable with one asset class, real estate for example, be aware that volatility must be within your comfort zone. If diworsification has not been a problem for you, consider diversifying into three asset classes to protect your sanity.

You also may have little time for investing. Investing in three asset classes will require more of your time unless you hire help.

Pay attention to any of your character flaws around investment professionals. Before you act on any advice, study the advice and compare it to what other advisors say, information in books, and any other well-researched sources of advice.

Remember, you are looking for emotionally compatible investments. Nearly all the advice out there is for investors uninterested in serenity. It is rarely appropriate for you. Always look at fees, expenses, costs, and taxes. Take your time. Go slow. It is your money. If you are not ready to make a move, tell your advisors to stop calling you. The best investment is the one that lets you sleep at night, not the one that lets your advisors sleep at night. A year or two with half your money in CDs is fine while you transition into your comfort zone.

Be aware that some investment professionals are not investing within their comfort zones. Some mutual fund managers have no idea what is their comfort zone. Fund complexes may assign rookie managers to run the most troublesome funds when they are only financially mature enough to be investing in treasury bonds. Some financial planners are in the wrong business. Property managers may make mistakes due to their incompatibility with real estate.

Before you turn any money over to financial professionals, make an estimate of whether or not they are investing in their comfort zone. Ask about their history of mistakes. If they have never made any mistakes, then they are in denial and clearly outside their comfort zone. For the mistakes they admit, determine if they will be repeated or can be overcome. For example, many mutual fund managers invested too heavily in tech stocks in the late 1990s. Those who took losses quickly and moved on likely learned from their mistakes and found their comfort zone. Those who held on, increased their stake, or rotated into other tech stocks are not learning. They are outside their comfort zone and in denial. Stay away from rookie managers and financial advisors who are not likely to yet know their comfort zone nor how to stay in it.

Buy and sell to establish your comfort zone

After completing an inventory and picking compatible investments, make the changes to your portfolio that are indicated. If you find this difficult, talk things over with your helper and with anyone who may be affected by the changes you intend to make including family members, coworkers, investment professionals, and others. With the consent and support of others, you will be able to move forward.

Once you have made the appropriate changes to your portfolio, stop and review your progress. You now know much about yourself. You have done an inventory and shared it with a friend. For most of you, many fun investment ideas are now apparent.

INDEX

ABOUT
THE AUTHOR

G illette Edmunds is the author of *How to Retire Early and Live Well With Less Than a Million Dollars*. He has appeared on *The NBC Nightly News* and AOL prime-time chat rooms and has been quoted in *Smart Money*, *Barron's*, *Fidelity Outlook*, *Mutual Funds*, *Bottom Line Tomorrow*, *New Choices*, *Third Age*, and *WomensFinance.com*, as well as on radio discussing the financial and emotional aspects of investing.

Gillette Edmunds began living off his investments in 1981 at the age of 29. As an individual investor himself, Gillette understands the feelings and inner struggles of other individual investors in uncertain markets. In 1991 he discovered a tool developed by a stock analyst, Bill Wilson, and a medical doctor, Dr. Bob Smith, to help people understand who they are and how that impacts investment decisions in their life. Since 1991, he has used this tool himself and helped others apply it to their own investments. *Comfort Zone Investing* is a simple, three-step explanation of this tool.

Gillette graduated from Stanford University in 1973, received a JD from the UNM in 1977, and an LLM in Taxation in 1978 from the prestigious New York University Masters of Tax Law Program.

Remembering his fears and resentments in the early 1980s and the devastation of the crash of 1987, Gillette hopes no reader of *Comfort Zone*

Investing will have to go through the painful self-teaching process and lessons he endured. Writing as an expert compatibility analyst of financial products and not a promoter seeking commissions and fees, Gillette believes his experience will keep those who follow him from making the costly financial and emotional mistakes he made and lead them directly to the serenity he now enjoys.

Gillette is married, has three children, and lives in Northern California. He writes every day and has a part-time investment consulting practice. He has served on the Board of Directors and done extensive public speaking for a non-profit organization. Contact him through his Web site, *www.TheRetiredInvestor.com*, where he will post free, bonus material for readers who need more information about Comfort Zone investing.